"Sarah Shin does what no one else has been able to do: connect a clear gospel summary with our stories of ethnic identity and reconciliation. I hope that not only all campus ministers but also every student leader in the country will read this book. I can't remember the last time I was so expectant for an upcoming book to arrive."

Doug Schaupp, national director of evangelism, InterVarsity Christian Fellowship, coauthor of *I Once Was Lost*

"Ignoring our diversity is not faithful to the Scriptures, the reality that we live in, or the future of the church. Sarah's experience as a minister of the gospel as well as her voice as a woman of color bring a unique perspective that is both deeply theological and richly experiential. What a gift it is to have a resource on crosscultural fluency that is crafted for the whole church."

Sandra Maria Van Opstal, executive pastor, Grace and Peace Community, author of *The Next Worship*

"How might Christian communities break away from the powerful grip of a colorblind narrative? By challenging Christians to reinterpret the significance and meaning of ethnicity through the lens of the good news of Jesus, this timely work points to a clear pathway forward that is biblical, pastoral, and prophetic. I strongly recommend Sarah Shin's work to all Christians who seek to better understand how our Christian and ethnic identities intersect in today's multicultural world."

Peter Cha, professor, Trinity Evangelical Divinity School

"In *Beyond Colorblind*, Sarah Shin offers us a personal and practical resource as we explore the issues of ethnicity, race, and diversity in our fractured world. This important book will prod at your heart at times, perhaps challenging you to reflect on your own assumptions. But it also serves to equip you—as a friend or neighbor, as a church or community leader, in work or in love. With humility, wisdom, and compassion, Sarah calls us to 'become *ethnicity aware* in order to address the beauty and brokenness in our ethnic stories and the stories of others.' Essential reading for today."

Jo Saxton, chair of 3DMovements, speaker, author of *More Than Enchanting*

"I will never forget hearing Dr. John Perkins say that if we want to disciple people in the Christian faith, a primary focus should be on stewarding ethnic identity. I also will never forget having no idea what that meant or how to do it! I wish I had *Beyond Colorblind* when I first heard those words. In this critical work, Sarah Shin lays the foundation for ethnic identity in a winsome manner and with a thoughtful approach. I'm convinced that when the light bulb turns on for the importance of ethnic identity, this book will become a can't-miss resource."

Daniel Hill, pastor, author of *White Awake*

"Beautifully written and astute. Sarah Shin takes readers on a deep, honest, and spiritual journey through the complications of our racial history. Along the way, she dismantles the objections of thin thinking and religious sentimentality while depositing a rich, nuanced, and healthy soil in its place. Whatever your background or level of experience in this conversation, Sarah's voice and wisdom will add rich texture to your understanding. I can't recommend *Beyond Colorblind* highly enough."

Ken Wytsma, author of *The Myth of Equality*

"Sarah Shin is brilliant! *Beyond Colorblind* is revolutionary; it is a prophetic, pragmatic, and plucky guide for recovering the gifts and blessings of our ethnic journey. Grounded in Scripture and empowered by personal narratives, this masterpiece is kingdom-focused, Christ-centered, and full of healing. Beyond being a 'must-read' book, this is a 'must-study' resource."

Emmett G. Price III, executive director, Institute for the Study of the Black Christian Experience, Gordon-Conwell Theological Seminary

"The unbiblical and unhelpful approach of being colorblind in a diverse world has resulted in significant unintended negative consequences that have adversely impacted the work of the multiethnic church. Sarah Shin calls us to move beyond our superficial understanding of culture, race, and ethnicity toward a more biblical theological approach that offers the hope of healing."

Soong-Chan Rah, North Park Theological Seminary, author of *Prophetic Lament* and *The Next Evangelicalism*

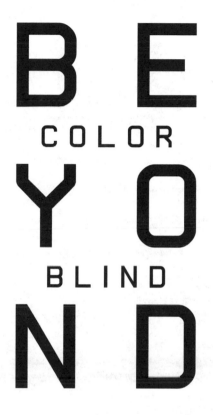

BE YO ND

COLOR BLIND

REDEEMING OUR ETHNIC JOURNEY

SARAH SHIN

IVP Books

An imprint of InterVarsity Press
Downers Grove, Illinois

InterVarsity Press
P.O. Box 1400, Downers Grove, IL 60515-1426
ivpress.com
email@ivpress.com

*InterVarsity Press® is the book-publishing division of InterVarsity Christian Fellowship/USA®, a movement
of students and faculty active on campus at hundreds of universities, colleges, and schools of nursing in the
United States of America, and a member movement of the International Fellowship of Evangelical Students.
For information about local and regional activities, visit intervarsity.org.*

*All Scripture quotations, unless otherwise indicated, are taken from The Holy Bible, New International
Version®, NIV®. Copyright © 1973, 1978, 1984, 2011 by Biblica, Inc.™ Used by permission of Zondervan.
All rights reserved worldwide. www.zondervan.com The "NIV" and "New International Version" are
trademarks registered in the United States Patent and Trademark Office by Biblica, Inc.™*

*While any stories in this book are true, some names and identifying information may have been changed to
protect the privacy of individuals.*

Figure 3 adapted from Edward T. Hall, Beyond Culture *(New York: Anchor Books, 1976). Iceberg image
© Lonely-iStockphoto/Getty Images*

Cover design: Faceout Studio, Tim Green
Interior design: Daniel van Loon
Images: Color abstract: © Luca Pierro/Stocksy

ISBN 978-0-8308-4515-6 (print)
ISBN 978-0-8308-8897-9 (digital)

Printed in the United States of America ∞

Library of Congress Cataloging-in-Publication Data
Names: Shin, Sarah, 1981- author.
Title: Beyond colorblind : redeeming our ethnic journey / Sarah Shin.
*Description: Downers Grove : InterVarsity Press, 2017. | Includes
  bibliographical references.*
*Identifiers: LCCN 2017042141 (print) | LCCN 2017041214 (ebook) | ISBN
  9780830888979 (eBook) | ISBN 9780830845156 (pbk. : alk. paper)*
*Subjects: LCSH: Ethnic relations--Religious aspects--Christianity. |
  Ethnicity--Religious aspects--Christianity.*
*Classification: LCC BT734.2 (print) | LCC BT734.2 .S465 2017 (ebook) | DDC
  277.3/083089--dc23*
LC record available at https://lccn.loc.gov/2017042141

P	23	22	21	20	19	18	17	16	15	14	13	12	11	10	9	8	7	6	5	4
Y	35	34	33	32	31	30	29	28	27	26	25	24	23	22	21	20	19	18		

To Shin, my husband.

You help me see and live in color every day.

CONTENTS

PART
ONE

REDEEMING OUR ETHNIC STORIES

BEYOND COLORBLIND

Michael, a twenty-four-year-old black man, was sharing with his small group about some hurtful experiences with racism that he had endured in the past year.

An elderly white woman tried to respond to his sharing with grandmotherly kindness.

"Oh Michael, when I see you, I see *you*. I don't see your color."

Michael didn't know what to say, so he said nothing. But internally he thought, *I'm a black man from Los Angeles. If you don't see my color, you might as well not see me at all.*

Using the paradigm of colorblindness, the woman was trying her best to affirm Michael's humanity and dignity. She was trying to say, "I'm not one of those racist people who thought color was a reason to degrade you."

But what Michael heard was invalidation: I don't see you.

Why did they miss each other?

THE LIMITS OF COLORBLINDNESS

In the past, seeing color meant believing that society should be unevenly and unjustly divided by color. Today, many see colorblindness as a corrective to the problems of racism and prejudice. People who are eager to separate themselves from overt racists like to declare themselves colorblind.

You might have picked up this book for one of two reasons: you believe in colorblindness, or you're disenchanted by it. If you're the former, you might see our present diversity in the United States and across the world as the triumph of a diverse, colorblind society. Colorblindness and diversity are celebrated in universities, workplaces, and churches alike. We elected a black president, not once, but twice. Surely these are signs of a post-racial society.

However, in 2015, a twenty-one-year-old white man killed nine parishioners and pastors that had welcomed and prayed with him at Emanuel African Methodist Episcopal Church, a historic black church in Charleston, South Carolina. When he was apprehended, the man confessed to wanting to start a race war between white and black. He was a self-proclaimed white supremacist.

This massacre is only one of the many stories of heartbreak and injustice affecting the black community. Trayvon Martin, Tamir Rice, Eric Garner, Michael Brown, and Sandra Bland have become the known names of black men, women, and children who died at the hands of white men and law enforcement officials who were not indicted. The public outcry against these and many other deaths of black Americans at the hands of police led to the Black Lives Matter movement. Some insist that education is the answer to eliminating racism, but our universities don't seem any better. In recent years, students vandalized Northwestern University's interfaith chapel with ethnic and homophobic slurs. Harvard Law School students placed strips of tape across display photographs of black professors. White dorm-mates at San Jose State bullied a black student, calling him the N-word and three-fifths of a person while repeatedly forcing a bike-lock chain around his neck. If education is the answer to racism, why do even our top schools seemed plagued by racial brokenness?

On top of this, Muslim Middle Eastern students at North Carolina State University were shot and killed in an altercation with a white neighbor in 2015. An Asian couple and a Puerto Rican man were gunned down by a white neighbor in Milwaukee for "not speaking English." The election campaign of 2016 exposed all sorts of rhetoric against Mexicans, immigrants, Muslims, and more. White nationalist movements are more visibly public. Similar nationalist, anti-immigrant, and anti-refugee mantras reverberate through Europe and the rest of the world.

We are not a colorblind society. These issues are not colorblind. They are racially and ethnically charged.

In a documentary about racial peace, Archbishop Desmond Tutu and Dr. John Hope Franklin discuss the colorblind issue. Franklin says there are people who think "we don't need to do anything about the problems that we have" and "just think colorblind and the problems will themselves disappear."[1] Tutu and Franklin assert that colorblind people have a hard time seeing the existing racial inequality and injustice. Individuals claiming colorblindness cannot address racial issues that they cannot see.

Naomi Murakawa, a professor in African American history, writes, "If the problem of the twentieth century was, in W. E. B. Du Bois's famous words, 'the problem of the color line,' then the problem of the twenty-first century is the problem of colorblindness, the refusal to acknowledge the causes and consequences of enduring racial stratification."[2] This might be why you are in the second camp of being disenchanted with colorblindness, because you've found that colorblindness does little to help dismantle existing injustice. In *The New Jim Crow*, Michelle Alexander helps document the reality that today the United States holds more black adults in correctional control (prison, jail, probation, or parole) than the total number of slaves that existed before the abolition of slavery.[3] It's slavery in the twenty-first century by another name. If you are part of an ethnic community that is struggling with the lasting effects of racism on your personal life and family, colorblindness isn't much comfort in your time of need.

The second point that Tutu and Franklin raise is that differences are not inherently bad. In fact, according to Tutu, "differences are not intended to separate, to alienate. We are different precisely in order to realize our need of one another."[4] Colorblindness seems to deny the beautiful variations and cultural differences in our stories. How would you feel if you shared something that's part of your Chinese, black, Irish, or Colombian background, and someone replied, "I'm colorblind!"? Blind to what? The food, stories, and cultural values that make up the valid and wonderful parts of who we are?

Colorblindness, though well intentioned, is inhospitable. Colorblindness assumes that we are similar enough and that we all only have good intentions, so we can avoid our differences. Given the ethnic tensions exposed by the 2016 election, we're seeing instead that our stories *are* different, and those differences cannot be avoided. Racially charged, ethnically divisive comments flood our social media outlets and news screens. Good intentions alone are ineffective medicine for such scars. The idea that we have transcended ethnic difference has been exposed as a mirage.

We don't live in a world that is in need of colorblind diversity because diversity that rests on colorblindness seems to lead to chaos. We need something beyond colorblindness, something that both values beauty in our cultures and also addresses real problems that still exist in our society decades after the civil rights movement.

THE SILENCE OF OUR WELL-INTENTIONED CHURCHES

Our churches often avoid the topic of ethnicity and race because we don't think it's relevant to our faith, or we're afraid of offending people and trying to avoid being "political." More often than not, we don't know how to talk about it and withdraw from conversations about race or ethnicity. We lack the skills, language, and understanding to be able to share the gospel in our diverse and divided contexts.

Perhaps the reason Christians have little to say is that, for a time, we bought into the secular world's gospel of colorblind diversity as the answer to our problems of ethnic division. Colorblindness often meant polite avoidance or silence, inside and outside the church.

Instead of being a prophetic voice, many churches also opted for colorblindness (see figure). In buying into colorblindness, we did not examine the Scriptures' rich depth of insight into God's creation and intent for ethnicity, and we lacked biblical literacy on the issue, leading to lack of theological reflection, formation, and repentance. Scripture formed no foundation for ourselves as ethnic beings. We either denied ethnicity as valuable or bought into the secular world's understanding of ethnicity. This robbed us of the opportunity to hear the stories of people who are ethnically different than us. We are shocked and unsure of how to engage when we hear of things such as a race-related incident or hate crime. Our lack of ethnic identity understanding for ourselves and those around us led to a proclamation of a gospel that is irrelevant or powerless in addressing real aches, pains, and questions. Racially and culturally unaware witness and involvement in our communities caused distrust; we sometimes did more harm than good and pushed people away from us—away from opportunities to hear the gospel and away from trusting Jesus. What resulted was and is a distant and often irrelevant, unaffected church.

The Christian story is one that acknowledges that we are fundamentally broken. Why would the realm of ethnicity and race be exempt from the influence of sin? Colorblindness mutes Christian voice and thought from speaking into ethnic brokenness.

Problems with Colorblind Diversity in the Church

- Lack of biblical literacy on ethnicity
- Lack of understanding self
- Lack of understanding others
- Irrelevant, harmful witness and stewardship that causes more harm and pushes people away from the gospel and from trusting Jesus
- A distant, ineffective church

In holding onto colorblindness as the solution, we as Christians are trying to doggy-paddle when we actually need to learn how to swim. We might sink in our attempts to stay afloat or cause others to drown as we thrash about in our good intentions.

Our world is in need of the gospel, a good news that goes beyond colorblindness that is not afraid of addressing ethnic differences. When it comes to ethnicity, our world needs Christian voices to call for change and reform with Jesus as the transforming center of it all. How can we relevantly live out the gospel in such a hotbed of emotions, scars, division, and chaos? If we avoid this topic now, we withdraw into ineffectual witness in word and deed. And we leave a broken and hurting world, friends and strangers, in chaos.

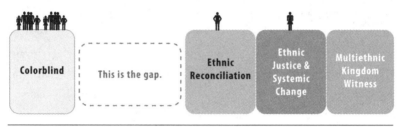

Figure 1. The colorblind gap

GOING BEYOND COLORBLINDNESS

When Michael was told "I don't see your color" by the older woman in his small group, he heard something like this: "I don't want to hear about or acknowledge some of the most beautiful parts of who you are ethnically and culturally, and I don't want to walk with you in the pain of what you have experienced racially."

This was a Christian-to-Christian interaction that yielded invalidation and distrust. How much more harm might have been done if this had been a conversation between a Christian and nonbeliever?

Suppose you find out that a friend was sexually assaulted or harassed. As you speak with the friend, you say, "I care about you and you're my friend, but talking about what happened to you makes me uncomfortable. So can we talk about all the other things we have in common and avoid this painful part of your life because it's awkward and uncomfortable for me? Thanks." What would your friend say? That's probably the end of the friendship because you're clearly not acting as a real friend. You're conveying that this friendship is about your own convenience and comfort—an act of selfishness and self-protection that bruises Christians and non-Christians alike.

Oscar Wilde writes,

> If a friend of mine gave a feast, and did not invite me to it, I should not mind a bit. But if a friend of mine had a sorrow and refused to allow me to share it, I should feel it most bitterly. If he shut the doors of the house of mourning against me, I would move back again and again and beg to be admitted.... If he found me unworthy, unfit to weep with him, I should feel it as the most poignant humiliation.[5]

Real friends aren't afraid of looking at a friend's real scars. And the scars that people experience in their culture, ethnicity, and race are places that need the gospel. Evangelism without real friendship and community without real concern for the needs of others is a hollow-sounding, empty gong.

Our ethnic scars are not always racial. Sometimes they are from idolizing things that our ethnic cultures prize. For example, in Asian cultures that emphasize family honor, honoring parents has often meant unequivocal obedience to the parents' dreams of financial success and prestige for their children, often at the cost of a child's dreams and desires. Language, worldview, and generational differences exacerbate some of the relational difficulties between parent and child. This, combined with something akin to the mentality of "saving face" for the family's reputation, can lead to broken family relationships, resentment, or mental health issues such as depression and anxiety. Non-Asian friends and pastors often try to counsel Asian Americans by giving them suggestions that are distinctly non-Asian, and these solutions end up causing more problems. Our ability to love and live out the gospel relevantly involves engaging the reality of ethnicity.

Instead of being colorblind, we need to become *ethnicity aware* in order to address the beauty and brokenness in our ethnic stories and the stories of others (see figure). But this is a road with treacherous ditches and potential roadblocks, and conversations full of tension, confusion, accusation, pain, and shame. Some of us represent the oppressed or the oppressor, ethnic enemies, strangers. We've seen conversations about race and ethnicity go south, real fast. What difference does Jesus make in this journey?

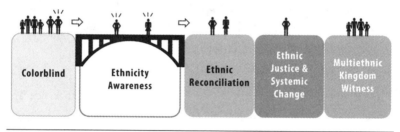

Figure 2. Ethnicity awareness fills the gap

KINTSUKUROI: THE ART OF RESTORING AND RECLAIMING

Pottery is an ancient and highly respected practice in Japan, and each vessel is made with great care and thought about the piece's balance, shape, and feel. With *Kintsukuroi*, the Japanese practice in ceramic art meaning "golden repair," broken pottery is repaired by setting it back together with an intentionally brilliant golden or silver lacquer. This method highlights each piece's unique history by emphasizing the fractures instead of hiding them. Often, the final work is even more beautiful than when the piece first came into being.

When Jesus shapes our ethnic identities, he is like the gold seam in Kintsukuroi. He demonstrates how each of us in our ethnic backgrounds and identities were made for good in the image of God, like beautiful pieces of pottery. But sin—in the form of cultural idolatries, ethnic division, and racism—causes damage, brokenness, and painful cracks in the story of our ethnic identities. When unattended, many of those cracks deepen into bitterness, prejudice, revenge, racism, hatred of others, self-hatred, depression, suicide, numbness, despair, and idolatry that we pass on to our children. God is not content to leave us to our brokenness, and he sends Jesus to redeem us in all of who we are. As children of God, we die with him in his crucifixion and rise with him in his resurrection.

Jesus' resurrection did not get rid of his scars. His scars remind us of the broken story of humanity and the powerful, costly love that came to save and mend us. As in Kintsukuroi, when Jesus enters our stories, the healing, redemption, and reconciliation he brings is the undeniably striking golden seam. Kintsukuroi doesn't deny the brokenness of the pottery—it uses it to tell a new story. Likewise, our scars become transformed by Jesus' scars. And it is the beauty of that story that allows us to share the gospel with those around us. We are most fully able to share the gospel when we can share about its impact on *all* of who we are. And when those diverse pieces come together as one body and share the myriad of stories of healing, reconciliation, and sacrificing for the other, we are a visibly powerful vessel of kingdom witness.

THE DREAM OF WHAT COULD BE

Kristin is a forty-year-old white ministry leader who spoke of the history of both abolitionists and slave owners in her family line during an outreach event. She apologized on behalf of white people to the people of color who had experienced racism from white people. She wasn't doing this because she was ashamed of being white; she knew that just as she represented the community of Christians to nonbelievers in the room, she also represented white people to the nonwhite people in the room. And she wanted to both preach the gospel and serve as an ambassador of reconciliation spiritually and ethnically. James, her thirty-year-old black colleague and close friend, also shared about his journey as a black man. Together, they spoke of how Jesus made them well and was healing them of lies, sin, racism, and brokenness, and they invited others to experience the same.

As a result of their discussion, a young white man named Erik became a Christian. Shyla, the black woman who had invited Erik to the event, wept as she watched Erik say yes to Jesus, not *in spite* of him being white, but *because of* who he is as a white man. Several black students also came up to Kristin, marveling, "I've never heard a white person talk like you before." One of them was Devon, a nonbeliever, who could barely find words to describe the Holy Spirit encounter he had during the time of closing prayer as Kristin had asked Jesus to bring healing to those who had experienced brokenness in their ethnic identities. "I don't know what happened to me," Devon said as he spoke of being flooded with warmth and the strange sensation of being deeply loved.

Kristin laughed and said, "I think Jesus happened to you."

Looking at her, Devon replied steadily, "Well, then you must have a whole lot of Jesus in you."

You must have a whole lot of Jesus in you. This was a comment from a non-Christian black man who was undeniably affected by the story of a white woman sharing about how Jesus was redeeming her ethnic identity as a Christian white woman.

This is a beautiful story—the dream of what could be. But how do we get there?

START BY NAMING OUR ETHNIC BACKGROUNDS

Just as the process of making Kintsukuroi art can't happen without distinct, identified pieces of pottery, the process of healing can't start until we name and acknowledge that we *all* have an ethnic background. Our ethnic identity and background is experienced culturally and racially in our context, in the languages we speak, in our family histories, and in the stories of our ethnic communities.

Ethnicity is more distinct and specific than *race* (Norwegian versus white, Taiwanese versus Asian). *Ethnicity* refers to common ancestry, tribe, nationality, and background, often with shared customs, language, culture, values, traditions, and history. *Race*, on the other hand, is the classification of people according to their supposed physical traits and ancestry. Race, though a manmade historical construct, has real-life present day realities. Power, access to employment and education, and social status historically have been unevenly applied to racial groups, leading to slavery, segregation, apartheid, and obstructed civil rights. For the sake of conversation, we need to be able to name and group people using commonly understood terms, even if those terms are limiting. Thus, this book will refer to continental groups of people by their racial categories (or in the case of Latino, their ethnic-cluster categories), which include ethnic diversity and also acknowledge racial histories and realities.

Black refers to those of African descent, including those whose ancestors were brought over as slaves (African American, African Canadian) as well as more recent migrants of the Caribbean (Haitian, Jamaican, Trinidadian, Barbadian) and Africa. A black American and a black South African have vastly different stories, though both of their peoples experienced racial oppression. They will have a different story from a Nigerian or Kenyan national who grew up as the ethnic majority or a tribal minority.

Asian refers to all of Asian descent, including the earliest Japanese, Chinese, Filipino, and Indian migrants to the United States as well as the later waves of Korean, Taiwanese, Lao, Cambodian, Bengali, Vietnamese, Hmong, Thai, Sri Lankan, and several other Asian ethnic groups. An Indian Canadian or Asian American have both ethnicities and nationalities that are integral parts of their story. They will have different experiences from Asians who grow up in Asia or other parts of the world.

Latino encompasses those who were annexed in during the formation of the United States as well as the great diaspora of Central American, South American, and Caribbean people from Mexico, Panama, Chile, Brazil, El Salvador, Honduras, Puerto Rico, the Dominican Republic, and more. Contrary to popular understanding, the US Census Bureau defines "Hispanic or Latino" as an ethnicity: "a person of Cuban, Mexican, Puerto Rican, South or Central American, or other Spanish culture or origin regardless of race,"[6] as Latinos can be white, black, brown, or other (for example, there are black Cubans, white Mexicans, Native Paraguyans, and everything in between). Some Latino communities use *Hispanic* and *Latino* interchangeably. Others prefer *Latino* because the "span" in *Hispanic* is a reminder of the colonizing legacy of Spain. To honor those who are uncomfortable with *Hispanic*, we will use *Latino* in this book.

Middle Eastern refers to those that are descended from the transcontinental region centered on Western Asia and Egypt, including countries such as Iraq, Turkey, Syria, and Iran.

Native refers to the hundred-plus tribes that exist today, including Pacific Islander and Hawaiian. Lakota, Navajo, Sioux, and Cherokee are a few of the many known tribes. *First Nations* is the name that Canada uses, which acknowledges the earliest presence of Native communities in North America.

White refers to those of the European diaspora, from the earliest Western European colonialists to past and present day immigrants from Northern, Southern, and Eastern Europe as well. Some white people can definitively trace their history back multiple generations, while others have so many different European ethnic heritages in them that "white" really is the best way they can describe their pan-European ethnic and racial background. This can feel jarring in particular to people who are not accustomed to thinking of themselves as "white" in their countries of origin.

White Americans have often thought of themselves as not having an ethnicity, as if *ethnic* is a politically correct term replacing *people of color*. But the Greek word *ethnos* means the nations, and we each are descendants of *ethnos*. This is true for those of us who are multiracial, who are adopted by parents of a different ethnic or racial group, or who resonate with being third-culture children (people who grew up in a culture different from that of their parents). None are excluded from the invitation to recognize their ethnicity and invite Jesus in.

When Americans of every ethnic background enter into a multi-ethnic community, they possess differing levels of understanding of their cultural and racial backgrounds. Black Americans tend to have more defined language for both culture and race, as both are talked about at the family dinner table. Asian and Latino Americans, by contrast, often have stronger self-identifying language for culture while they vary in having language for a racial identity. Add white Americans into the mix, and you have a people who often lack self-identifying language for culture and race. The first conversation about race is disorienting for white people, as it usually involves learning about racial oppression caused by whites. The result is a *double deficit*: lack of cultural identity and a negative racial identity.

When you have a room full of people who have varying levels of language, experience, and awareness, a conversation about ethnicity and race is difficult. It's like trying to run a marathon with a group of marathon veterans alongside sprinters, casual joggers, and couch potatoes. It makes for chaos, misunderstanding, and a good measure of frustration and heartache. There is a great need for understanding our own stories for the sake of our individual stewardship and witness as well as the corporate witness of an evangelistic community.

We need to fully know our stories in order for Jesus to fully do his work. To use a Kintsukuroi analogy, if I were a blue teacup that has experienced brokenness and cracks, my hope is *not* to be made into a gold-veined green vase! The Potter made me into a blue teacup, and Jesus delights in restoring me to be what I was meant to be. He heals my blue teacup cracks so that I can share my restored story with others.

HOW JESUS SHAPED MY ETHNIC STORY

I remember coming into college very aware of the faults of my Korean American culture, and in particular, its destructive anger. I grew up hearing stories about how Japan had occupied, mistreated, raped, and pillaged Korea. I felt that scar on Korea's consciousness and saw that hatred in many Korean families. I was raised and bred to resent Japan. I watched destructive arguing, stubbornness, and divisiveness plague my family and realized with horror that I too was full of damaging anger—at the family brokenness, the poverty we'd faced, and the racism my parents endured. I watched Korean American classmates start race-based arguments with other ethnic groups at my public high school in New Jersey, causing division even among the Asian community. The phrase "make like a Korean church and split" was something that I and many other Korean American churchgoers regularly experienced. Many left the church, disillusioned.

By the time I got to college at the Massachusetts Institute of Technology, I was nearly ready to reject my ethnicity, or at least to label it as impossibly broken forever. The Asian and white churches of my youth never addressed the reality of racial tensions that existed in my high school nor the realities of cultural idolatry and family brokenness that tore apart many Asian immigrant families. Faith seemed divorced from reason, and if reason existed, it didn't acknowledge my culture. I was tired of being part of an irrelevant faith that seemed powerless to address the real issues my non-Christian friends and I were facing.

To my surprise, I found myself drawn to a group of believers who were dominantly Korean American but were working hard to reach out to their Asian American friends (as well as white and Jamaican).

I floundered in multiethnic spaces because I didn't know how to operate in them. I didn't know what it meant to be a Korean American Christian. But with this group of women and men, faith was not only comforting, it was also compelling. They talked regularly about what it meant to be Asian American and follow Jesus, and about how to pursue hospitality together and break down dividing walls between Korean, Chinese, Taiwanese, and Japanese people. White men and women speakers shared about their own journeys in engaging race and ethnicity. Black ministry leaders spoke about engaging racial injustice and poverty. We talked about the challenges of honoring our Asian parents while not agreeing with all of their values; we discussed forgiveness and healthy conflict resolution versus the falseness of "saving face and pursuing harmony" at any cost.

It was here that I was challenged not just to follow Jesus on Sunday but also to submit my whole life, including my Korean American family and its pain, to Jesus. I asked him to renew my family instead of assuming that my parents, like other Korean parents, would always be broken. It was pivotal in helping me learn to have a real relationship with a father with whom I clashed so much. Jesus was healing my relationship with my father, and I didn't have to become a white Christian for this to happen. After I sent my father a photo album expressing my love and gratitude for his many sacrifices, my mother told me that he spread that album out on his desk and wept for hours. Our relationship had been so broken, but Jesus was helping both of us heal.

My friend Paula, a Chinese American agnostic, opened up to me about her own life as I shared with her about how Jesus was changing my relationship with my father.

"You should try praying and asking God to show up," I said.

"You think he'd listen even if I'm not a Christian?" she asked.

"Yes," I responded with confidence, while silently praying, *It's on you, Jesus, if she doesn't hear back!*

Slowly, she started praying and asking Jesus for help, and slowly, she started to see real changes in how she and her mother were relating to each other. Years later, I got an email from Paula saying that she had decided to become a Christian and was getting baptized in the Pacific Ocean.

"I wanted to tell you," she said, "because you were the first person that told me about Jesus."

I wept when I got that email. Paula had grown up in Alabama, where the only time God was mentioned to her was when church-going Christians told her she was going to hell because her family was agnostic. When she saw that the gospel had relevance to her family story—her ethnic story—she gave Jesus a chance.

THE IMPACT OF JESUS REDEEMING OUR ETHNIC STORIES

We need to recognize what we are meant to be in our ethnic stories and identities so that we can ask Jesus to restore us. It's not just about being racially aware and sensitive so that you can be a crossculturally savvy navigator of a multiethnic group. It's also about Jesus redeeming and restoring our ethnic identities, which makes for a compelling narrative that causes non-Christians to ask us about our faith as they wonder, *how could that kind of hope and healing be available to me?*

When Jesus interacts with the Samaritan woman at the well in John 4, she responds with astonished cynicism: "You are a Jew and I am a Samaritan woman. How can you ask me for a drink?" (John 4:9).

Jesus' attempts at conversation are parried by the woman's multiple pointed questions about their people's historic ethnic tensions. But by choosing to speak with her, Jesus the Messiah is embodying what Israel was meant to be: the priesthood nation and light to the Gentiles. He is redeeming what it means to be an Israelite Jew. And as the Samaritan woman experiences Jesus redeeming his people's ethnicity, she starts to desire such living water. Jesus is transforming the disciples' understanding of what it meant to be Jewish and the Samaritan woman's understanding of what it meant to be Samaritan. Ethnicity no longer serves as the confines of mission. It becomes the vehicle, the sacred vessel in which God's story comes to light.

Our ethnic stories rarely form in isolation; they often involve encounters and altercations with those around us. It's knowing our ethnic stories and the ethnic identity narratives of those around us that helps us realize the complexity of values, scars, trigger points, and words to avoid. It helps us know more how to sensitively share the gospel and boldly invite even those that were considered ethnic enemies or strangers to become believers.

Knowing and owning our ethnic narratives helps us understand the real issues of injustice, racial tension, and disunity that exist in the world. Ethnicity awareness helps us ask the question of how to prophetically engage in pursuing justice, racial reconciliation, and caring for the poor while we give the reason for our hope: Jesus, the great reconciler of a multiethnic people.

Elizabeth, a young white college minister with InterVarsity Christian Fellowship at Smith College, experienced healing as she learned about her ancestral German and English heritage, her family's communication and conflict styles, and how her family had responded to race and other ethnicities throughout its history. She came to know that she, as a white woman, was made for good by God. Elizabeth also experienced powerful forgiveness as her black and Asian colleagues prayed forgiveness and blessing over her and her people. Something changed for Elizabeth in hearing that she was made precious as a white woman (as our society tends to view white culture either as blank or defined by white privilege only) and that she was forgiven for what whiteness has historically represented in the past. Elizabeth was commissioned to live differently and follow Jesus in a new way as a white woman. After hearing the news of black men, women, and children dying at the hands of police in multiple incidents during the fall of 2014, Elizabeth and other InterVarsity leaders felt convicted to create a prayer space for black students, even though black students didn't usually attend their group.

To the leaders' surprise, five black women showed up. Elizabeth asked the women to share about how the leaders could be praying for them, and the women opened up about their heartache, questions, fears, and deep grief. After an hour of weeping and praying together, the women remarked that though they had been to many university events in response to what was happening to the black community, this was the first time anyone had actually asked them how they were doing.

Because of the time Elizabeth spent exploring her own racial and ethnic story, she could reach those who were hurting and engage in their stories. She was not afraid of their stories, nor was she afraid of the historical friction that her story would uncover as it intersected with their stories because she was part of the great reconciling story of Jesus. The black women who attended the prayer space began asking how they could better reach secular black students who needed to hear about the gospel during this difficult time. Experiencing this kind of hospitality and intentionality helped them turn their eyes toward witness. Compassionate engagement in ethnicity and race led to the opening of new doors in evangelism and reconciliation.

For me, Kristin, and Elizabeth, God turned the chaos of our experiences of ethnicity and race into something else. He transformed our ethnic identities to be the vehicle of sharing the gospel.

THE INVITATION IS YOURS

No matter your ethnicity, Jesus wants to do the same with you. He wants to sanctify the space of your ethnic identity, show you where you are made in the image of God, and heal you of brokenness so that your ethnicity becomes the vehicle of mission to a broken and chaotic world. The stories I share are just some of the many I have had the privilege to hear as I train ministry leaders about engaging ethnicity, reconciliation, and evangelism in InterVarsity Christian Fellowship and other church and Christian institutions. Regardless of age, gender, ethnic background, or class, I've found that it's essential for individuals and communities to recognize that we each have an ethnic identity.[7] A helpful tool I use is evangelist Dr. James Choung's framework for explaining the gospel called the Big Story, summarized below:

- *We are designed for good:* we must recognize the beauty inherent in each of our ethnic identities.

- *We are damaged by evil:* we must recognize the effects of sin, brokenness, idolatry, prejudice, and racism in each of our ethnicities.

- *We are restored for better:* we must invite Jesus to show us what is beautiful and what he wants to heal in our ethnic identities.

- *We are sent together to heal:* we must invite others to drink of the living water of Jesus so that many more can hear the good news and share that news in witness, justice, and reconciliation.[8]

This framework is accessible to non-Christians and Christians alike, and it helps people pinpoint where they are in their ethnic journeys. Some have never even considered their ethnicities, while others have been trapped in places of pain or confusion. The eighteen-year-old and the septuagenarian alike can have conversations about their very different experiences. The Big Story framework allows for discussion of spiritual, physical, social, emotional, and racial dimensions of one's ethnic journey.

We are trapped behind the futility of colorblindness or the helpless impotence of our good intentions unless we choose to recognize that our ethnicities are the sacred vessels in which God wants to bring healing and redemption. We cannot be sent out with the gospel of grace unless we experience that for ourselves.

To those that would try to avoid the topic, stigmatize it as a liberal agenda, or succumb to despair, the powerful counter-response is that ethnic identity redemption and reconciliation are at the heart of the gospel. God created us for good, but cultural idolatry and racial brokenness tore apart our intended multiethnic community. Jesus came to restore us, redeem us, and release us for his kingdom mission, not in *spite* of our ethnicities, but *in* our ethnic identities. For example, if you are a white man or woman hoping to share Jesus with a black community, you need to know their context *and* your context in order to be able to share the gospel in a transformative way. Sharing the gospel is never about being safe or polite. It's about loving deeply, and you can't love what you do not know. Simultaneously, you need to not be defined by fear and shame and thus avoid opportunities to share the gospel. It's not enough to say, "Don't be afraid"—as bravado is not a good witness. If you know your own story as well as the story of the people you want to reach, and you humbly share a relevant gospel, you are a powerful witness.

So, in the name of hope, learn and own your ethnic identity story. The first half of this book focuses on learning your ethnic story and inviting Jesus into that space so that you can proclaim the kingdom of God. The second half focuses on how to share that story and how to steward your ethnic identity in multiracial, multiethnic spaces. Join me in exploring how Jesus amplifies the beauty and excavates the brokenness in each of our stories and unleashes those redeemed stories to better share the gospel.

QUESTIONS FOR INDIVIDUAL REFLECTION AND SMALL GROUP DISCUSSION

1. What messages about colorblindness did you grow up hearing?

2. The author argues that colorblindness denies persistent race-related problems as well as beauty in our ethnic differences. How does this compare with your own experience and the experience of your loved ones?

3. What is your ethnic background? Be as specific as possible. How long has your family lived in this country?

4. As you learn more about becoming *ethnicity aware*, what questions, fears, and hopes are stirring within you?

RECOMMENDED READING

"Be Color Brave, Not Color Blind," TED blog by Mellody Hobson

Beyond Racial Gridlock: Embracing Mutual Responsibility by George Yancey

Can We Talk About Race? And Other Conversations in an Era of School Resegregation by Beverly Daniel Tatum

Disunity in Christ: Uncovering the Hidden Forces That Keep Us Apart by Christena Cleveland

"A Journey Towards Peace," PBS interview with Desmond Tutu and John Hope Franklin

True Story: A Christianity Worth Believing In by James Choung

White Awake: An Honest Look at What It Means to Be White by Daniel Hill

InterVarsity Christian Fellowship has a *Beyond Colorblind* video series about ethnic identity. For a video that introduces the conversation, go here: http://2100.intervarsity.org/resources/beyond-color blind-overview.

2

ETHNICITIES MADE FOR GOOD

While leading a training session on ethnicity, I spoke of how every ethnicity was created for good before it was damaged by sin and evil. We heard from Asian, black, and white staff who shared about how God had taken them on a journey of showing them what is beautiful and broken about their ethnicities.

Near the end of the session, we prayed for the white people in the room. Prompted by the Holy Spirit, several of the black leaders prayed for "our precious white brothers and sisters" that they would know they were created in God's image, intended for good. After these words of kindness were uttered, I saw stunned silence and heard a combination of soft crying and gasps of surprise from our white brothers and sisters.

Later, several white women and men remarked with astonishment that they had never heard the words "white" and "precious" used together in one sentence. "Is that even allowed?" one asked. Given that much of the secular world engages in talking about race and ethnicity by talking about the damage done by European Americans, they were bewildered by this gracious pronouncement of goodness. It seemed undeserved. And yet it reflects the character of God, who looks upon all of us and calls us into the image we were made for.

Too often, we enter into the conversation about multiethnic community through the lens of what is wrong. But this is not how God starts his story. Genesis starts in an entirely different way—with a word of kindness and graciousness: "Let there be light."

THE AFFIRMATION OF GOD IN GENESIS 1

In the beginning, God created the heavens and the earth. Genesis 1 describes in different thematic days how the earth was created by God. "And God saw that it was good" is a reverberation that repeats at the end of each day. It is repeated when Genesis describes the creation of the stars and moon, the lights in the sky. When God creates the birds, fish, land animals, and vegetation, you see a great diverse ecosystem emerge, according to all of their kinds. When humankind is made, the poetic narrative gets very particular about its details:

> Then God said, "Let us make mankind in our image, in our likeness, so that they may rule over the fish in the sea and the birds in the sky, over the livestock and all the wild animals, and over all the creatures that move along the ground."
> So God created mankind in his own image, in the image of God he created them; male and female he created them. (Genesis 1:26-27)

While all other elements of creation seem to have been from an *ex nihilo* (out of nothing) kind of formation, the birth of humankind is modeled after an existing image: God himself, who has community within the Father, Son, and Holy Spirit. The triune God can't help but love because it's in his nature, and creating more out of that perfect love is the only natural response.

Because man and woman are made in the image of God, they are made to receive that perfect love from God and to reflect that community to each other. And after a resounding echo of "it was good" that follows every day of creation, God's delight is emphasized after his creation of man and woman in his own image: "it was very good." In Genesis 1, humanity is the pinnacle of creation.

Have you ever had your ethnicity affirmed by another as *good*, without having to even describe why, but just because God made it so? I remember the first time I heard the words, "You are a gift to this room because of all the beauty and leadership you bring in a distinctly Korean American way—fiery, humorous, tenderly aware of who is in the room, and yet unwilling to back down from saying what needs to be said." I was unaccustomed to hearing my ethnicity being described in a way that was not about being the "other." I had wrestled to own the assertion that I too was American, despite not being white. Understanding that God made me *good* as a Korean American woman allowed me to face the brokenness that existed in my ethnic identity and community.

We hear God's deep, fatherly voice of love in the beginning of Genesis and see that we were created for good in who we are as humans. A wise seminary professor once said to me with impatience, "I hate when Christians sigh and say, 'Well, we're only human.' To be human is to be made in the image of God. Sin is the thing that makes us un-human; it undoes the image of God that was placed in our DNA. Only Jesus can restore us back to our intended humanity." To be made human is to be made beautiful, in the image of God.

HOSPITALITY AND STEWARDSHIP

We reflect God's image, the *imago Dei*, not because we stand on two legs or have higher intelligence than animals, but because we were created to have community with each other. We were made to model the hospitality of God to another as we have communion with God himself. Men and women are created to rule over the fish, birds, animals, and all the earth. We are God's vice regents, appointed to have dominion over creation and reflect God's character, values, and community.

We have a hard time understanding the word *dominion* without cringing because our experience of people with power sometimes includes corruption and abuse. But the way it was intended in Scripture is different. Genesis 2:15 reads, "The LORD God took the man and put him in the Garden of Eden to work it and take care of it."

Taking care of the garden, of creation, was how humans were meant to have dominion, to use power and leadership for *the care and flourishing of all*. Genesis 2, being specifically a story that celebrates the creation of man and woman, shows us how God created us for community, as it was "not good for the man to be alone" (Genesis 2:18). A *helper*, a word in Scripture that means one who saves with strength and is used to describe God throughout the Old Testament, was created in the form of woman. And Adam delights in having a partner as he and Eve tend to the garden together. They are naked, and they feel no shame. This is not just a celebration of marriage. It's a celebration of intimate human community, of loving trust and mutual respect that reflects the Trinity's communion within itself. The *imago Dei* is reflected in how we practice hospitality and stewardship of who we are so that creation itself may benefit.

Later in Genesis, humans begin to multiply and fill the earth. Just like the biodiverse animals and plants of creation, people spread out according to different tribes with culturally distinct ways of living, such as those who live in tents and raise livestock (Genesis 4:20), those who play stringed instruments and pipes (Genesis 4:21), and those who make tools out of bronze and iron (Genesis 4:22). We read about maritime people who spread out into clan territories, as well as warriors who built kingdoms and cities (Genesis 10). They have multiplied and filled the earth according to their clans and languages, territories and nations. These details in the lineage of Adam's descendants are important enough to be included in Scripture. Ethnicities, with distinct cultures and languages, are being created.

DEFINING BEAUTY IN ETHNICITY

Each of us has an ethnicity that God made for good, an ethnicity that is beautiful in its distinctive particularities. Our ethnic identity is the backdrop in which God displays his goodness and creativity. We are made well in our specific and God-given ethnic backgrounds, not in spite of them. Someone is not beautiful *though* she is black or African American; she is beautiful *in* her blackness, in a way that can only be expressed in the shape and shade of her face, skin, and heart.

It is common to hear adages such as "beauty is only skin deep" or "beauty is in the eye of the beholder," but this kind of beauty is not what we are talking about here. Beauty is not the world's definition of sexual attractiveness or impossible-to-gain standards of thinness or fitness. Beauty is how we reflect the image of God. It is possible to say that black is beautiful and simultaneously affirm the beauty in our white or Native or Asian or Latino brothers and sisters. There is no one ideal standard of beauty in ethnicity in God's eyes.

So many cultures prize a certain standard of physical beauty in men and women, and all suffer when they try to fit into such impossible and subjective standards. Human secular standards of beauty hailed in magazines and movie screens are often dehumanizing; they reject the way God made us. Instead of having our human subjective biases form our understanding of beauty, we should have the image of God form our lens for understanding beauty. It's when we reflect the image of God and his intentions for us that we are most beautiful.

EMBRACING OUR ETHNIC BACKGROUNDS

Each of us has an ethnicity that God made well, whether we are descended from a long line of Germans or Indians; or have pan-European, pan-Asian, pan-Latin, or pan-African ancestry; or are multiracial; or are adopted by a family whose ethnicity differs from our own. God made no mistakes in his creation. These are non-negligible parts of our identities, even if we have been told that they should be hidden, forgotten, assimilated, rejected, or disregarded. And there was no mistake in how God made us, though many of us bear the marks of the brokenness of the world in how we experience those ethnicities.

In the gospel story, we see an affirmation of our ethnic identities, no matter who we are. Whether we are Hmong, Trinidadian, Venezuelan, Polish, English, Sioux, or Egyptian in ancestry, God invites us to embrace who we are. An Indian American friend of mine, Ritu, found that embracing the right way to say her name (Rid-thoo) brought her deeper pride and willingness to share her culture and ethnic heritage instead of apologizing for her less "common" name. One young man, who identified as white and grew up in the South, told me about how his grandmother was Malaysian and that his family and even he himself would laughingly poke fun at it in passing. His Malaysian heritage was seen as inconvenient and even uncomfortable because of its assumed animistic spirituality. Once he realized that ethnicity was affirmed and valued in Scripture, he shared, "I realize now that God is saying that my Malay side is not negligible and that it is an important part of who I am. And he's inviting me to relearn what I tried to forget."

We often forget that Jesus himself was part Moabite and that Matthew takes great pains to show us that the story of Ruth was an important part of Jesus' heritage and story. Matthew carefully includes the mention of Tamar and Bathsheba (Uriah's wife) in his account of Jesus' ancestors, reminding us that prostitution, adultery, and murder are also part of the Jesus' family history. In addition, Timothy, Paul's young protégé, is part Greek and part Jew, and it's certainly not negligible as they both consider how to help Timothy navigate an ethnically complicated Roman empire.

Some of us might not know about our ancestors beyond a couple generations. Some of us might have complex, painful, or shameful parts of how our families came into being (especially those that have the legacy of slavery, war, or rape in the family story). Jesus doesn't ignore this but instead is set on redeeming those hurtful stories.

People who were adopted by parents of a different ethnicity have the complex reality and task of recognizing and honoring the goodness of the culture they grew up in as well as their ethnic heritage. Examining Moses' story, we learn that he was reared as a prince in the Egyptian courts for the first forty years of his life and then lived as a shepherd in the wilderness of Midian for the next forty years. Moses' Hebrew heritage is important, but so is his Egyptian upbringing and culture as his story plays out when God chooses him to lead his people to the promised land.

I recently met Kaylyn, a young Korean American woman, at a mostly Asian gathering of ministers. We talked about what it was like to lead as Asian Americans. She was nervous as she said, "I'm adopted, and I grew up in a white family. I never feel like I belong at these things." I looked at her and said, "Of course you belong here." To me, her face and how she walked felt distinctly Korean, though she had not grown up connected to her ancestral culture. Though some Asian cultural expressions might not make sense to her, she was having distinctly Asian experiences of race, and such a space was important for her to experience so that she could lead in more fruitful ways. Her adoption didn't erase her ethnic heritage. In owning her ethnic heritage along with her adoptive white family's story (a journey that took much time and prayer), Kaylyn was able to also more fully own her adopted story and identify with adopted people.

We're all at varying points of understanding our ethnic identities, especially from the perspective of the gospel. If you don't know where to start your journey, say to Jesus, *Show me how you want to write your story in this part of my life, in my ethnicity.*

Eddy is Armenian American, and he came to the United States from Lebanon when he was ten years old. He is descended from a people that have been a diaspora community since the Ottoman

Empire. In Lebanon, Eddy was the minority because he was not Muslim nor Arab. He knew he did not belong there. When he came to the United States, the feeling of not fitting in continued. Everything in him wanted to assimilate as quickly as possible, but he hated the summer months because his skin would become noticeably darker than that of neighbors and friends. He would vigorously scrub his skin in the shower, hoping that it would change his complexion. He was embarrassed of his parents' accents and how loudly they talked and the fact that they drank and smoked (which was perfectly acceptable in Armenian culture but not in most white churches). Eddy attended a mostly white church, and he internalized that the way to be clean and right before God was to be white.

He thought college was his chance to become free from his family and to fully be white. He went on a summer missions project to Asia where his small group leader, a white woman, asked him about race and ethnicity. Eddy answered, "Ethnicity doesn't matter to me because Jesus matters more." She replied, "That makes me really sad." Her response shocked him, because he thought he had given her the "right" answer. It led him on a journey of figuring out what was wrong with his theology.

The following year, Eddy was mentoring a young Latina leader who had recently become a Christian. She asked him, "How do I figure out what it means to be Latina and Christian?" He had no answer, no framework to even begin to understand her question. He realized that she was asking, "How do I hear God in my own heart language?" But he did not even know how to answer that question for himself. His answer had been to become white and to reject his culture.

God led Eddy on a journey of reaching out to more Latino students. He began to understand how to develop contextualized tools so that Latino students could hear Jesus' invitation for them without having to reject their Latino-ness. This meant that Eddy had to know more of who he was, to understand how God spoke to him in his "heart language," and to see himself as wonderfully and beautifully made in his Armenian heritage, not in spite of it.

As Eddy continued his leadership in campus ministry, he began to reach even more communities with the gospel, including the black community. Now a forty-year-old man, Eddy often gets asked, "What's the secret to your success in reaching young black men and women, people who are a completely different ethnic and racial group than you?" His response is simple: "Know and love who you are. The key is not becoming an expert at black culture. I don't listen to most of the music or get the jokes and movie references. I build trust, but not because I know the latest hip hop artist. I build trust because I know who I am, and my black students respect that authenticity. They know I'm not trying to act a part—people in general can sniff out imposters quite quickly." Eddy's work in leading men and women of every ethnicity isn't to get them to be like him culturally—it's instead helping them be fully who they are.

God breathes his Holy Spirit into our ethnic stories for the sake of mission. We must open ourselves up to his words of kindness, to his greeting and affirmation of who we are in our ethnicities. One of my colleagues, John, was a forty-five-year-old Irish American man when he started his ethnic identity journey. As he was praying, he was startled to hear Jesus speak to him in a Gaelic accent. "Did you not think that I would speak to you in the heart language of your people?" he heard Jesus ask. Many American people hear Jesus speak to them in their heart languages, be it Spanish or Chinese, affirming that God is not the God of the Western world but of the whole world.

EXPLORING OUR CULTURAL DISTINCTIVES

Once we become open to seeing our ethnic identities as intentionally and beautifully made, we can ask the question of how God shows us his image in the values and expressions of those cultural backgrounds. Each of our ethnicities has distinctives, cultural particular expressions, of how we live out the *imago Dei* in our hospitality toward others and our stewardship of who we are.

It's important to note the difference between uniqueness and distinctiveness. Hospitality, for instance, isn't a unique trait of one culture. However, every culture has distinct ways of expressing hospitality. Some do it by giving lots of hugs and kisses, some do it by respecting personal space and privacy. Some say, "make yourself at home" and do away with decorum, while others go to great lengths to honor you as a guest. Hospitality bears different flavors in different cultural vessels.

I met my high school friend Felicia, a fun and friendly Puerto Rican American, in art class. In my school, you didn't have too many in-depth friendships beyond your own ethnicity. I wasn't quite sure how to take either her questions that showed a genuine interest in me or her insistence on sharing who she was. I learned the proper Latina way to say her name (Fel-lee-cee-a instead of Fel-lee-sha), and she taught me how to salsa and merengue, much to my chagrin and the bemusement of the art teacher. Felicia didn't see me as an "other"; I was becoming part of her family. She didn't even think twice when asking me to New York's Puerto Rican Day parade. (My bewildered Korean parents refused. Why would a Korean American go to such a parade?)

When I met other Latinos and Latinas later on in life, I realized that there was a beautiful common thread, a cultural distinctive about Latinos: *familia*. I've experienced the common phenomenon and gift that Latinos bring in their willingness to adopt anyone that is not blood-relations into their family. The warmth, celebration, and willingness to fully include a stranger is very distinct from my Korean understanding of family, which is also hospitable but more reserved in welcoming others (and where honoring elders and relationship with elders plays a much more prominent role). Felicia flung wide open the doors of hospitality and modeled loving the stranger in a whole new way, full of passionate living and fun. Yet Felicia was often rejected by her peers for not being "Latina enough"—meaning, she didn't have only Latino friends, she did well at school, and she spoke Spanish with a Puerto Rican accent. Felicia remarkably cast off all those false assumptions of what it meant to be Latina, and she shared the best of her culture with me. I am forever grateful.

My friend Stacy, a Mexican American and gifted ministry leader, shared about going to college after growing up in a part of Los Angeles that was 97 percent Mexican American. She was used to being part of a larger group and rarely saw herself individually in terms of her gifts or what she had to offer the kingdom, especially as a woman. Elizabeth, her white campus minister, helped her see her gifts when it came to hosting and leading a flourishing Bible study. Stacy said, "The gift Elizabeth gave to me was her understanding of the stewardship of the individual: leadership, voice, discipleship, and mission." For Stacy, being taught to value her individual self and voice allowed her to bless her *familia* even more.

Thinking of individualism as a gift is surprising to some. There are scores of sociology, anthropology, and race books that talk about the damage Western individualism has done in multiethnic settings. But it's one of many ways that God expresses his *imago Dei*. Soong-Chan Rah writes, "One of Western Christianity's greatest contributions is the possibility of experiencing the grace of God on a personal and individual level."[1] There is something beautiful about the Good Shepherd who values the life of a single sheep in the flock of ninety-nine. Individual stewardship is a gift and cultural distinctive of many white Americans. Used for kingdom purposes, it draws us deeper into prayerful individual intimacy with God and to obedience and faithfulness in mission.

Many white Americans, especially those who are distant from when their families first immigrated to the United States, grow up being encouraged to speak up about ideas, politics, and policies, and to use their individual voice particularly in the world of ideas.

Stewarding their individual voice, ideas, money, and work is emphasized as part of being a responsible member of society. Particularly
if they are from middle class to affluent means, white American
children are told to hope and dream with abandon, and that they can
be whatever they dream if they work hard and apply themselves.
White American parents sacrifice so that their children can be independent, autonomous, and self-reliant. Independence combined
with hope leads to individual contributions to society (as parent,
neighbor, teacher, doctor, etc.). Stephen, a white American man who
works with Latino and Native communities, said, "A distinctive of
white people is that we dare to hope and to go to places we have
never been to before."

White friends have shared with me and other Asian American
friends how we challenge their understanding of what it means to
honor their parents. While the independence emphasized in white
culture helped them transition more easily into adulthood, our white
friends saw in us a commitment to honoring our elders and parents
despite generational cultural clashes. Asian immigrants often sacrifice
so that their children don't have to suffer and can be safe and secure,
which is in contrast to white parents, who want individual freedom
and autonomy for their children even if there is some risk of failure.

Honoring the other is one of the highest values in Asian communities, be it a parent, family member, friend, or guest. It is the most
important part of being hospitable to the other. Asian Americans
often complain that it takes half an hour for a big group to figure out
where they want to go eat because they want everyone to be happy
with the choice. It took me many years before I would believe friends
who said it was okay to show up empty handed at their house because
I was taught that it's imperative to honor your host. This kind of
group-think and group-honoring-mentality can be incredibly hospitable and loving, especially if you're entering a new environment or
exploring faith for the first time. I've seen several white and black

friends join an Asian community because they were deeply struck by the hospitality and inclusion of the other that they experienced in such a context.

One of the most powerful gifts given to me by another culture was from the black community. I'm Korean American and the granddaughter of a military general. My ancestors, who had been invaded and conquered, raped and pillaged, were seen as an inferior race by the Japanese government in centuries past. Anger is a common reality for the Korean people. There is also a fatalism, a cyclical form of thinking that can give way to despair, bitterness, and a passive acceptance of suffering. Instead of fighting for change, there can be a defeatist attitude of "this is the way it will always be."

It is in my black churched friends that I started to hear a different way of engaging with suffering. The black church in America rose out of the legacy of slavery, but instead of accepting sorrow and injustice, a different refrain came out of the people: Jesus is coming, and in his kingdom, suffering will one day end. In the black community, there is a willingness to acknowledge suffering but also a prayerful and prophetic refusal to believe that this is the way it will always be. As a young woman, I saw the way black women in the church are respected and honored and the way that voices can be used to pronounce powerful and prophetic change. Leadership is encouraged in folks at a young age. I saw a vision of who I could be as a woman of God that was compelling and beautiful because I heard a different refrain and answer to the question and dilemma of sorrow. Joy and perseverance in suffering is a powerful cultural distinctive that I have witnessed in the black church over and over again.

My friend Josh, a black pastor, shared honestly that it's hard for him to name how black Americans with slave ancestry were created for good because the "creation" of black Americans who descended from enslaved peoples is inextricably tied to the kidnapping, violence, and rape that were crucial to their formation. Josh added that there are many beautiful ways black people have redeemed that experience of suffering; however, it doesn't make the genesis of the black American story any easier to hear. Indeed, even with such broken beginnings, we see God's originally intended goodness and creativity shine through the cracks of our nation's history. While black Americans don't have a monopoly on creativity, their contributions to artistry have brought incredible depth to music, the visual arts, dance, and more in American culture, history, and theology.

My friend Alysia is a nationally respected black spoken word artist. For our wedding, my husband and I asked her to perform a blessing comparing marriage to the faithfulness of Ruth to Naomi. There was not a dry eye in the house by the end of her performance, and there was a proclamation of the gospel that was powerfully heard in her poetry in ways that could not be reproduced by a sermon.

The African diaspora is very diverse, and as we start to understand the culture of black African and Caribbean brothers and sisters, we see even greater depth and beauty. The same is true of the Latino experience, the Asian diaspora, the European diaspora, the Middle Eastern diaspora, and the multitude of Native American tribal backgrounds.

Many of us may not know Americans that identify as Native American (or you might know that you have Native blood but know very little about what it means). In Native American culture, there is a deep appreciation and respect for nature. Their stewardship and regard for creation permeates many of their customs, rituals, and celebrations. In Native time, you are done when the event has run its due course. Time slows down from the busy industrialized, mechanized lives we are accustomed to. There is a peace and holism that exists in this kind of attention to each other.

Rashawn, a Navajo friend, led a group of us on how to better cross cultures to reach out to Native people. He spent almost an hour having us introduce ourselves and our families on both our mothers' and fathers' sides. You could feel our confusion at how long it went. He later explained, "You just learned how to enter Native culture, to be aware of people and their stories, to not be pressed by time. This is what it means to enter into Native people's stories and Native people's time. For those of you who aren't familiar with this, it might have felt like a waste. But for Native people, this is everything." Rashawn was modeling for us how to steward time and also host Native people well.

It's also in Native theology that we find a distinctive place of affirmation for our multiracial persons. Richard Twiss, a Lakota Christian theologian, shared the pithy response of a tribal woman who was told by a young man that he was part Native. "Which part," she asked, "your leg? You either are or you aren't."[2] There is no compartmentalization of self into disparate parts in Native consciousness. In a world where multiracial people are often told that they are broken halves or parts of an incomplete whole, this kind of cultural perspective is a gift and a challenge to a society that often defines individuals by what they are "mostly made up of" or by which ethnic community accepts them as their own.

If we were to try to describe the differences between all of the ethnicities listed and (not listed) here, this chapter would have to be its own book. It would need to be updated every couple of years because culture is ever changing and responding to its environment and context. The stories are like still-shots from an incredibly long movie reel that is playing, with historic turns and moments that shape the past, present, and future. We live in a rainbow of ethnic backgrounds that we can try to ignore in an attempt to affirm our "sameness." But in doing so, we deny the chance to embrace who God has made us to be, and we cut ourselves off from understanding the beauty of how God made the other. We become inhospitable guests and hosts in a multiethnic world that needs to hear the gospel in a culturally relevant, not colorblind, way.

Your invitation is to embrace your ethnic identity and to hear God's voice of kindness and affirmation of how he made you. When you know who you are, you will be able to learn about the distinctive values, expressions, and characteristics of your culture that reflect his image. Then you will be better prepared to help others know who they are as beautifully created, ethnically diverse women and men of God.

QUESTIONS FOR INDIVIDUAL REFLECTION AND SMALL GROUP DISCUSSION

1. What are some common things you grew up hearing in your family about what it means to be your ethnicity regarding family, money, time, perseverance, sacrifice, education, and so on?

2. What are some beautiful things you have appreciated about your culture? Where have you seen hospitality, love, care for the other, and powerful expressions of worship emerge among your people?

3. What are some beautiful things you have appreciated about other cultures? Where have you seen hospitality, love, care for the other, and powerful expressions of worship emerge among different ethnic communities you have been a part of (not just seen on TV)? How has it affected how you view your own culture or values?

4. Take a moment to thank God for making you in your ethnic background. Ask him to show you more of the beauty and story of your people. Listen to see if he gives you a verse or image of hope. End with a Scripture reflection on Psalm 139:13-16:

For you created my inmost being;
   you knit me together in my mother's womb.
I praise you because I am fearfully and wonderfully made;
   your works are wonderful,
   I know that full well.
My frame was not hidden from you

when I was made in the secret place,

when I was woven together in the depths of the earth.

Your eyes saw my unformed body;

all the days ordained for me were written in your book

before one of them came to be.

RECOMMENDED READING

Being Latino in Christ: Finding Wholeness in Your Ethnic Identity by Orlando Crespo

Being White: Finding Our Place in a Multiethnic World by Paula Harris and Doug Schaupp

Black Man's Religion: Can Christianity Be Afrocentric? by Glenn Usry and Craig S. Keener

Living in Color: Embracing God's Passion for Ethnic Diversity by Randy Woodley

More Than Serving Tea: Asian American Women on Expectations, Relationships, Leadership and Faith edited by Nikki A. Toyama and Tracey Gee

InterVarsity Christian Fellowship has a *Beyond Colorblind* video series about ethnic identity. For a video about the beauty in our ethnic identities, go here: http://2100.intervarsity.org/resources/beyond -colorblind-beauty.

3

THE CRACKS
IN OUR ETHNICITY

Charlene is Ghanaian American. Her father told her from a young age that assimilating to her white surroundings was the way to success. "You have to work twice as hard and be twice as good to be seen," he'd say. During kindergarten, she went to the bathroom and washed her hands under the running water for several minutes trying to "get the black off." In first grade, she heard a friend call her brother the N-word. When she asked him why he used that word, he replied, "That's what my dad calls you people." She realized at a young age that even if she tried to be colorblind, the world she lived in wasn't.

In the beginning of Genesis, God is like an exuberant artist, a potter, proudly displaying his work. Gleaming fresh from the Creator's kiln, vibrant with color, humankind is meant to reflect God's image in its communion with each other. But sin enters the picture in Genesis 3, where the serpent successfully tempts Eve into trusting something else to be like God. He tells her that the fruit of tree of the knowledge of good and evil will make her like God, but this is a lie. Only communion with God will help us live out the *imago Dei*. This first sin of Adam and Eve—the distrust of God and idolatry of something else—drives a high-impact crack into the pottery art of what God intended. It's the kind of fissure that leads to more cracks, as death, envy, murder, division, polygamy, and all other kinds of brokenness enter the story of humanity.

Definition of Terms

White supremacists refers to white individuals who engage in racist speech and racial violence against nonwhites (and often against Jews and LGBTQ people). They often see the United States as a nation intended for whites.

White supremacy, on the other hand, is the idea that white people are inherently superior in intellect, beauty, character, culture, and ability. It exists in multiple systems and attitudes in schools, corporations, churches, and communities, where the "white way" of doing things is seen as normative or the standard to which all should aspire.

Privilege, in contrast, is the phenomenon where advantages or immunity are granted to or enjoyed by certain persons beyond the common advantage of all others. In the case of *white privilege*, racial privilege can yield things such as shorter prison sentences for a criminal offense or family financial support that makes education, entrepreneurship, and home ownership more accessible. This differs depending on the economic background of the white person (someone descended from a family with money versus someone from a family with generational poverty). Thus, a black or Latino American from an affluent background might have more economic privilege than a white person who has been living in poverty. However, the black person will have to navigate subtle and overt racism no matter how wealthy they are, whereas the white person will not.

For further explanation of these terms, go to beyondcolorblind.com.

In the table of nations in Genesis 10, we read about people groups that later will be at war with or enslave the Israelites (Egypt, Canaan, Aram, Babylon, and Assyria). And the cracks set in humanity ripple even further, causing the oppression and destruction of ethnic groups at the hands of others. Every major civilization was built on the backs of the people it oppressed, be it Japan's conquest of Asia (and its twenty-million-person holocaust), Europe's colonization of Africa and South America, the Aztec empire's military campaigns to acquire daily human sacrifices for its temple gods, the decimation of Native communities in North America, or slavery and segregation in the United States. Slavery, ethnic superiority, and the setting up of laws benefitting one people group at the expense of another all rest on the idea that one people can be supreme, or like God, above another. Japan carried out its belief of its ethnic supremacy in how it conquered, killed, and raped Koreans. America was founded upon the idea that European men were created equal by God yet Natives were expendable, "savages" and black Americans were "three-fifths" human. Such systems of white supremacy (as compared to white supremacists, meaning skinheads and Neo-Nazis) seem hard to shake. Today, we see the effects of unequal drug-sentencing that favors white offenders, biased and dangerous police treatment of black Americans, and rampant racism found on college campuses, in sports teams, work places, and presidential campaigns. Movements such as Black Lives Matter and Black on Campus are protesting these systemic and unchallenged unjust practices.

On top of this, the United States (and the rest of the world) is full of a hitherto unimaginable kind of ethnic and global diversity. We have Hmong, Cambodian, Sudanese, Congolese, Colombian, and Croatian recent immigrants who have fled war, genocide, ethnic cleansing, and their own experiences of systemic injustice and division. Still other immigrants represent the majority and the privileged in their society (consider the Han Chinese, who make up 90 percent of China even though there are more than fifty ethnic minority people groups in China). A Ugandan or Haitian American might have very little in common with a Black American in understanding cultural or racial experiences. A more recent Chinese immigrant is not going to share much with a Chinese American who has been in the United States since the days of the earliest railroads.

The difficulty of this chapter is trying to give framework that allows us to examine the cracks in our ethnic backgrounds in such a diverse context. But we need to, or else our cracks will deepen or we will unintentionally or willfully cause more damage. We can't ask Jesus to heal us if we do not know what we need healing from in the first place.

And we can't steward ourselves in a multiethnic world if we don't realize our own places of pain first. Broken responses to that pain are found in idolatry, racial and ethnic division, rejection of ethnicity, defining ourselves by our scars, and self-punishment.

BROKEN RESPONSE NUMBER ONE: IDOLATRY

Idolatry can look different in various cultures. For instance, in Asian cultures, children are taught to either treat their parents as secondary gods or to become gods themselves, pursuing success, financial gain, and the envy of their community. Imperfections, particularly public imperfections, are not tolerated. "Swallowing bitterness" is a common Chinese saying, where one is expected to endure suffering in silence. But that makes it difficult to bring up conflict or address relational or mental health issues, resulting in long-term bitterness, resentment, family division, depression, and broken relationships. The National Alliance on Mental Illness reported in 2011 that "Asian American teenage girls have the highest rate of depressive symptoms of any racial, ethnic or gender group."[1] According to the Asian American Psychological Association, suicide is the second leading cause of death for Asian Americans aged fifteen to thirty-four.[2] Between 1996 and 2006, thirteen of the twenty-one suicides at Cornell University were Asian American students, although they made up only 14 percent of the student body.[3]

No one can stand the pressure of being someone's god: it either distorts the would-be god or its worshipers. In ethnicity, the beautiful distinctives of a culture often become the very things that get distorted.

In Latino cultures, men are often seen as more important than women. Daisy, a Latina friend, explains that "machismo can become *machista*," an exaggerated sense of power. The prizing of masculinity can often lean to misogyny and unhealthy behaviors including adultery, domestic violence, or alcoholism. Women in traditional Latin American households are taught to not speak up and are restricted in their individual freedoms, while their male relatives are free to express themselves and do what they want (in the United States, this disparity lessens with subsequent generations). Combined with issues of poverty (especially in recent migrants), injustice, and racism faced by Latinos, the *familia* breaks down.

If you were Satan, would you not delight in breaking apart the most beautiful aspects of an ethnicity's culture? Would you not try to get Latinos to reject their ethnicity because of their pain and also get the surrounding society to view it only by its scars and brokenness? I spoke with a young Latina who said, "I don't know who I'm mad at: non-Latinos who have said and done racist things toward me, or Latinos who keep telling me that I'm not really Latina because I speak American-accented Spanish and have friends who are non-Latino. I feel stuck between resenting being rejected for being Latino and also wanting to reject my people because they've rejected me."

For white Americans, there is a high regard for individual merit, self-earned hard work, and dependence on educational background. When such things become idols, it makes it difficult for white people to understand how our justice systems don't afford the same merit or work opportunities for nonwhites. The influence of the Enlightenment and church culture creates an allergic reaction to the slightest hint of moral failure (much in the way that family-shaming imperfection is avoided in Asian contexts). Whether in shame, disappointment, or disgust, many white Americans leave churches that feel devoid of the grace of the gospel. Those who value being educated or enlightened often are eager to seem informed in conversations about race or ethnicity but then will often be the most unforgiving toward other whites who don't have the equivalent education or similar crosscultural experiences. A black friend who was disturbed at watching white activists unsuccessfully woo less-informed white people remarked, "One of the most unpleasant people to be around is the angry white person who is furious at his own people for not getting it."

White people who understand the racism their friends of color experience are often those most impatient with their own people; they look down on other whites as uneducated, ignorant, or racist. And being called a "racist" is a cardinal sin among many college-educated whites. You can call a white person selfish, arrogant, rude, but call them a racist, and they react like you just spat in their face. Individual enlightenment seems to be the goal, but individual enlightenment does little to actually change a society. And if enlightenment is an idol, then you're essentially fighting racism with an idol. You can't win against the enemy using his tools. It is instead a self-promoting pat on the back, an accolade to individual moral achievement. It is self-worship.

Idols are dangerous because we often don't recognize them and therefore can't see that they cause brokenness. Idolatry separates us from God because we trust something other than God. When the angel of the Lord appears to Gideon and tells him to tear down his household gods, Gideon does so in secret in the middle of the night, afraid to challenge to his family's idolatries in broad daylight (Judges 6:25-27). When our idolatry is unacknowledged or unchecked, it damages us, the people in our communities, and other people.

BROKEN RESPONSE NUMBER TWO: ETHNIC AND RACIAL DIVISION

While idolatry can be subtle, the signs of ethnic division are more visible in how they affect us today. An Armenian friend once remarked that it's impossible to ask an Armenian about their ethnic background without hearing about the Turkish genocide. Being Armenian becomes "the one Turkey has sinned against." The same goes for black Americans and Native Americans in the United States, who today feel the effects of the legacy of slavery, genocide, and racism. As a Korean general's granddaughter, it's impossible for me to ignore the repeated attempts at conquest and oppression by Japan in the country of my ancestors.

We may expect all Latinos to get along, but in reality, differences in language, culture, and history exist. Do not get a Mexican American mixed up with a Puerto Rican, or vice versa. Pakistan and India are not friends, and those prejudices carry over to this side of the globe. Italian, Irish, and Eastern European Americans were labeled as "colored" in the earlier half of the twentieth century and were thought of as less intelligent, lesser in moral character, and thus less human than their Western European counterparts. It's a great mistake to assume that black Americans will get along with Haitian Americans or second-generation children of African immigrants. Nigerian Americans often share about how they grew up with other black children deriding them for their Nigerian heritage and culture. This caused strong resentment either of black Americans or of their own ethnic backgrounds.

Ajit, a research scientist with a doctorate degree, works for a pharmaceutical company. He is an Indian American whose parents immigrated to the United States in hopes of having greater opportunities than in India, where they were part of the lower castes. However, one of the managers at the pharmaceutical company was also Indian American, only she was a descendant of the highest castes and resented Ajit due to his family's caste. Verbal berating, prejudice, and insults were a regular part of how she interacted with Ajit behind closed doors. How do you fight this type of enmity and bigotry that has existed for hundreds of years?

Such experiences of historical conflict, systemic racism, or personal ethnic prejudice and racism can leave deep scars in us. And our broken response is often to define ourselves by our scars and to define others by their scars.

BROKEN RESPONSE NUMBER THREE:
REJECTION OF ETHNICITY

Once we get past the barrier of colorblindness, we are confronted with other potential barriers. We can be tempted to define our ethnicity by the ways we or our people have rejected others or been rejected by others. Instead of the image of God informing our understanding of ethnicity, human divisions and values serve as broken standards. Miroslav Volf writes that evil "keeps re-creating a world without innocence. Evil generates new evil as evildoers fashion victims in their own ugly image."[4]

Hatred of the other. Given the historic nature of ethnic tension, conflict, war, and racism, it becomes accepted in cultures to define their ethnicity by their hatred of an ethnic group. Black men are told, "Don't you dare bring home a white girl." When Melissa, a Mexican American, dared to marry a Puerto Rican man, her father refused to speak to her for twenty-five years, relenting only when her mother was suffering from cancer.

Viewing a people as inferior. It's an unfortunate reality that people are labeled by their negative stereotypes or projections in media. "All Mexicans are lazy" is the stereotype when in reality many Mexican Americans are hard-working and diligent. Even if one would never admit to viewing a people as less than, our implicit hidden biases say much. Julian, a black pastor, was serving on a team with another black pastor who recognized that Julian was holding back from confronting sin patterns in white male students. He asked, "Why is that, Julian?" After some conversation and reflection, Julian realized with surprise that though he was Ivy-league educated and prized for his intellect, he had unconsciously bought into the belief that he had less authority over white men because he was black.

Viewing a people as superior. When ethnic superiority is a view held by those in power, unjust systems and restricted access to power for others can result. Often times, African and Caribbean Americans view nonblacks as more ideal marriage partners or friends than their own people. Or, in the case of Asian Americans who ask to be treated "as white people," they don't realize that instead of challenging an unequal society, they are aspiring to be included as part of the privileged racial group. They add to the problem instead of challenging the premise of superiority. For example, when a jury indicted Peter Liang, a rookie New York city police officer, for the fatal shooting of a black father named Akai Gurley, the Chinese American community protested across the country, divided even among itself. They demanded that Liang either be given the same privileges given to white police or that Liang should receive a proportional sentence and not be made into a scapegoat for the pressures put on the law enforcement community.[5]

Hatred of the self. Sometimes, the impact of either cultural idolatry or experience of racism (or both) can cause someone to despise their ethnicity. Many Asian Americans, Latinos, black Americans, and others try to associate with something other than their ethnicity because of those experiences. For white Americans, the historic and current scars caused by white Americans can cause them to despise their ethnic identity and whiteness. Self-hatred can cause people to lament that they are trapped in the cultural idols and expectations of their ethnicity—and feel like there is no way out other than to bow down to the gods within.

Rejection of the ethnic self. Hatred of self can lead to a desire to disavow one's ethnicity. Many times, for nonwhite Americans, this can lead to a disavowing of their background of color because they "basically feel like a white person." Or, some white Americans can try desperately to try to absorb another ethnicity's culture and experiences in the hopes of not being "without a culture anymore." Multiracial people have the complex and difficult task of trying to figure out who they are; they often represent two ethnic groups or races that have historically been at war with each other. Someone who grows up biracial black and white can feel like they have to choose—which side do they embrace? Multiracial people sometimes choose to view a certain part of their ethnic background as negligible or unredeemable. Often, they are told that they are broken pieces of a whole that can never be. They are rejected by both sides because they represent the other. Ultimately this can lead to the rejection of one's own people.

BROKEN RESPONSE NUMBER FOUR: DEFINING OURSELVES BY OUR SCARS

And if we do not reject our people or those considered "not our people," our temptation becomes to define ourselves by our scars. Racism has had real effects on many people of color, and in particular the black American and Native American experience.

Black Americans suffered brutality, the breakdown of the nuclear family, the degradation of their bodies as vehicles of sexual procreation only, and division even against each other to curry favor with the "master." The end of slavery did not bring an end to this cycle; the lynching period post–Civil War to the mid-nineteenth century continued the brutalizing of black bodies, the false and base stereotyping of black men as sexual beasts, the destruction of black families, and the reign of white supremacy. In today's outcry against the death of unarmed black men, women, and children at the hands of law enforcement, we hear an eerie pattern of white police officers testifying that they were afraid for their lives because of the aggression they perceived in the black men they shot. Inequity exists, even today. One in three black American men are incarcerated, often given harder sentences for drug-related crimes that occur at the same frequency as their white counterparts (but with lighter and shorter sentencing).[6] Black drivers are more likely to be pulled over than white drivers.[7] Those stats are true whether the driver is African American, Jamaican, Nigerian, Haitian, or multiracial black.

Today, black people are called epithets and racial slurs, implied to be less than others at work or school, and suffer the indignity of painful interactions with the police, with neither a doctorate degree nor a clerical collar making a difference in how they're treated. Experiencing this regularly can cause several reactions in black men and women: exhaustion, numbness, anger, shutting down, post-traumatic stress disorder, depression, fear, and suicide.[8] How does one *not* define oneself by the reality of these scars?

James grew up being told, "Be black and be proud!" This affirmation of blackness contradicted the message that black men were inferior, undesirable, or less than when compared to nonblacks. James grew up watching and experiencing racism personally and in his black community. He wondered what it meant to be black. Was it to try to fit in? That didn't seem to work. Was it to be angry all the time? That didn't really seem to be a long-term option either, as he watched many friends become depressed and consumed by their anger. Jeremy, who is descended from both Nigerian and black American families, often withdrew as a response when confronted with racism and the N-word. He didn't want to be the "angry black man," but he also didn't want to be subjected to further abuse. Caught between two bad options, he learned to shut down to protect himself.

I've watched a number of Asian Americans, Christian and not, reject or resignedly accept the relational dysfunction with parents and family without even questioning whether it could be another way. Curiously, Asian churches, much like Latino or black churches, might affirm their ethnic heritage but do little to challenge the negative parts of their culture. We sometimes passively accept things as they are because we have a broken understanding of our ethnicities. "He's just being Irish," or "she's just being Puerto Rican," becomes our dismissive response when defining our ethnicities by brokenness.

Native Americans paid great costs at the hands of white superiority. Courtland, a Lakota friend, shared this analogy from Navajo theologian Mark Charles: the Native people are like a grandmother who invited guests into her home. They wanted her bedroom, so she ended up sleeping in the guestroom. But they wanted that too, and she ended up sleeping on the couch. But they wanted that too. So with nowhere to go, she went up to the attic, invisible to the quarreling guests below who refuse to visit or honor her.[9]

Native Americans are a people who suffered being torn from the land with which they had a deep connection and commitment to steward. Their families and villages were decimated by disease and war, and they experienced the indignity of being seen as subhuman hundreds of times over in broken treaties and unjust policies. Today, we falsely are taught that Native Americans are a thing of the past. At a conference I attended, a Navajo man named Rashawn softly pleaded with the group: "Please don't forget us. We are still here." His soft-spoken and sincere words pierced us. It's not enough that Native Americans remember who they are. He is asking non-Native people to remember, to counter the scar of being forgotten.

When your people have been oppressed for centuries, it becomes normative in that culture to hate the oppressor, just as the Jews hated the Romans and the Samaritans, their ethnic enemies, far worse. Lack of forgiveness becomes like a tumor that festers and grows inside, making it difficult for anything else to have room. And without the gospel, not forgiving and even vengeance makes sense. What rational person could forgive slavery, lynching, genocide, or racism? Nowadays, the secular world's response to historical racial injustice and violence is to use rhetorical violence in how we speak to those with power. Are there any options other than retribution? "Love your enemies" is the most unfathomable command in all of Jesus' teachings because it rubs against our desire to have an "eye for an eye." Without the cross and resurrection of Jesus, there is no rationale for forgiving the other. And the next logical step is to ask ourselves: Is there an ethnic group that we are choosing to not forgive?

The reality of the fall is that each of our cultures has experienced sin and evil. As a result, we can define our view of our ethnicity by its scars: I'm the sin, or I'm the sin done to me. And our view of other ethnicities can also be to define it by its scars. If we lean on our own human ability to heal, we can be tempted to either reject our ethnicities because they are broken or to conform to our people's assumed cultural norms.

BROKEN RESPONSE NUMBER FIVE: SELF-PUNISHMENT

A fifth broken response can be to try to make up for the mistakes of one's people. Self-punishing penance is different from penitence (genuine sorrow for wrong doing) and just reparations (payment for wrong doing determined by a court or judge). It's different from Catholic practices of reflection that help lead to deeper repentance and forgiveness. Self-punishing penance tries to atone by inflicting harm on oneself. This is particularly evident in white Americans who wrestle with "white guilt" or "white shame" after learning about the history of American racism and systemic injustice. The reality of what happened in the policies of justice, business, housing, law-making, military action, and more is staggering. For the white American navigating such conversations, it can be extremely disorienting as they begin to question all of what they've known to be true.

I've seen many white Christian ministry leaders, activists, and laypeople stay deeply committed to justice and reconciliation work between ethnic communities—and yet there is a lingering phenomenon of fear and anxiety about making mistakes and a sense of shame about the history of whiteness in America. Guilt is different from shame, as guilt is the awareness of wrongdoing that leads to conviction and repentance. Shame, on the other hand, is the sense that one is irreparably, irrevocably broken.

Many friends and ministry colleagues of color have commented to me, "I'm sick of white people feeling bad for being white." I've watched white men and women in their twenties, thirties, and forties remain committed to racial justice though they lose their sense of commitment to Jesus. They are trying to do penance on behalf of the sins of their people. Self-punishing penance is works-based righteousness that doesn't lead to life. It kills the soul.

If that resonates with you, the bad news is that nothing can atone for the legacy of slavery and racism. Jesus calls us to care for the poor, stand up for the oppressed, and invite the lost to the kingdom, but such an invitation is based on an obedience of hopeful faith, not crippling shame. The good news is that there's hope offered in Jesus, who reconciles all to himself and to each other. But we need to come to him with full awareness and knowledge of our cracks first.

PAUSING TO LOOK AT THE CRACKS

No ethnic group has been exempt from the effects of sin. No ethnic group is unaffected by patterns of idolatry and interracial and intraracial brokenness. We live in the reality of the scars and idolatries that make us bow to the idols that are worshiped in our ethnic cultures. We turn blind eyes to the people who end up suffering because of racism and prejudice, or we tolerate racial hatred, prejudice, rhetorical violence, and vengeance toward the other. We are unable to even recognize the areas where we need to ask Jesus to come, transform, and restore. As a result, we are unable to "love God, and love neighbor" fully because we have not examined our blindness. We need to pause and look at the cracks.

Confession. Our response must be the opposite of what Adam and Eve chose in the garden. Instead of hiding in the bushes or refusing to name the sin, we must confess the places of cultural idolatry, prejudice, self-hatred, superiority, hatred of the other, and racism that have affected how we understand our own ethnic identities (and the ethnic identities of others). Confession in community is powerful because the public naming of sin unmasks the sin, and it begins to loosen the secret hold it has in one's heart. Many times, confession about ethnicity will involve confessing the sins of our people, whether it's racism committed by our people or the idolatries that we follow unchecked. Confessing those sins means that you are praying as someone interceding for one's people, just as Moses, Isaiah, and many other prophets did. Instead of giving up on your own people, you're stepping in and asking the Lord to be among you.

Lament. Mourning and grief is scary for many of us, and yet that is the proper response to hearing about sin and the pain that sin causes ourselves and others. Cultural idolatry, ethnic division, and racial brokenness have caused the generational pain that we see today. Lament is the invitation to come before God and say, "This should not be!" We were made for life, not death, and all signs of sin and death should make us say, "No, this is not the image of God!" It should not be that our culture causes harm to women and children because of its idolatries. It should not be that cultural idolatries cause us to choose our own success and gain at the expense of others. It should not be that racism, ethnic division, genocide, and slavery entered the world. It should not be that we are gripped by shame, fear, hatred, depression, despair, and division.

In this season of racial turmoil and pain affecting the black American community, I've been struck by how few black Christians have had the chance to lament and mourn with Jesus about their community's pain. Lament wasn't an alternative they considered or were offered. It's one thing to feel despair, anger, or depression on your own about the state of the world. It's another to say, "Jesus, weep at this tomb with me." This lament can be quiet or loud, tearful or reflective, angry or wordless. God can handle our real responses of grief. Having led lament prayer with young adults and ministry professionals around the country, I've heard this consistent response from black women and men: "I didn't know I hadn't lamented until we started praying, and then everything I was carrying, trying to be strong, came down as I just wept. Before, my heart was just numb. I needed to mourn and invite Jesus into my grief, or else it was just going to crush me."

Repentance. When John the Baptist calls people to repent and be baptized, he is inviting people to turn from their old assumed norms and to choose a different trajectory. Confession and lament over *specific* sin and its *specific* effects is to be followed by asking Jesus to show us a different way of living out our ethnic identities. We are repenting of previous choices of color-blindness, rejection of self, hatred of others, and bowing down to our cultural idols. Repentance is saying, "Jesus, this doesn't work. Can you show me a different way?"

Particularly in the case of forgiving an ethnic enemy, it can be difficult to forgive. One can start with saying, "Jesus, I surrender to you my lack of forgiveness. I don't forgive, and I don't want to forgive. But I want to want to forgive."[10] The honest naming of the cracks and confession of our inability to heal ourselves invites the Holy Spirit into these broken spaces.

WHEN WE WEEP WITH JESUS

Last year, I was in a room full of ministers who were engaging in lament prayer over ways that racial brokenness affected our respective ministries. As I prayed next to some black colleagues, I heard the Lord say, *Pray with Tony using the words* oori ahgah ("our precious little one" in Korean).

But Lord, I objected, *Tony doesn't understand Korean.* Jesus responded, *That's okay; just do as I say.*

I knelt down next to Tony and told him that I was going to pray for him in Korean. Tony, who was quietly praying by himself, nodded. And as I began to weep and say those words in Korean, something broke in Tony, and he began to weep, crying out to the Lord about the pain he was experiencing in his body, the pain of the race conversation, and the pain of being an orphan from the housing projects of Chicago. I was not expecting the kind of emotional lament that came out of

Tony. But when he and I debriefed later, he was filled with wonder as he told me what the Holy Spirit was saying to him in that space of lament: *I am your Father. You are my beloved child.* It was exactly what the Lord had been saying to me, though I was repeating the same four syllables in a language Tony did not understand. The Holy Spirit used Korean to speak to Tony and minister to his scars.

Jesus wanted to weep with Tony; he wanted to say, *I see you, your pain, your wounds, your scars. And I want to be next to you, to touch your scars bringing healing, comfort, and hope.* He wants to do the same with you. Will you let him?

QUESTIONS FOR INDIVIDUAL REFLECTION AND SMALL GROUP DISCUSSION

1. What are some broken responses that you have had to your ethnic identity?

2. Where have you seen idolatry in your own ethnic people? Were there any mentioned in this chapter that resonated with you? How has that affected you, your family, and/or other people in your ethnic group?

3. What are experiences of ethnic tension or racism that have affected you, your family, or those close to you?

4. Find some others who are willing to engage in confession, lament, and repentance with you. Read Psalm 14 or 51 together as you pray.

RECOMMENDED READING

America's Original Sin: Racism, White Privilege, and the Bridge to a New America by Jim Wallis

Between the World and Me by Ta-Nehisi Coates

The Making of Asian America: A History by Erika Lee

The Myth of Equality: Uncovering the Roots of Injustice and Privilege by Ken Wytsma

The New Jim Crow: Mass Incarceration in the Age of Colorblindness by
    Michelle Alexander
*The Next Evangelicalism: Freeing the Church from Western Cultural Cap-
    tivity* by Soong-Chan Rah
Prophetic Lament: A Call for Justice in Troubled Times by Soong-Chan Rah
White Like Me: Reflections on Race from a Privileged Son by Tim Wise

InterVarsity Christian Fellowship has a *Beyond Colorblind* video
series about ethnic identity. For a video about the brokenness in our
ethnic identities, go here: http://2100.intervarsity.org/resources
/beyond-colorblind-brokenness.

4

ETHNICITIES RESTORED FOR BETTER

My friend Josh, a pastor, picked up the microphone in a room full of black men and women and said, "I am a black American, descended from slaves. But more than that, I am descended from a people who prayed for freedom and found it from a God who freed them."

You could hear the intake of breath and ripple effect of that statement in the room. Josh was not denying the painful history of his black ethnic identity. He was not denying the deep wounds of slavery and racism. But he was defining the scars of his people by the scars of Christ. And somewhere in that rang a clarion call of hope. It was the story of Jesus, gleaming in the cracks of the anguish of Josh's ethnic background.

Jesus knew ethnic scars. He lived in a time when ethnic tensions and vengeance bubbled over like a hot cauldron. The Jews resented Rome, which punished and crucified hundreds if not thousands of those who tried to rise up against its regime. And civil war, betrayal, prejudice, and ethnic hatred had separated Jews and Samaritans for more than six hundred years (see Josephus, *Ant.* 18.29-30; 20.136). And yet Jesus treated Samaritans with kindness and healed those who did not share his ethnic background.

My friend Josh was no stranger to pain. He was often the only black kid at his school in an almost all-white Iowa town where his dad was a doctor at the local hospital. When he was little, he was bullied almost every day for being black, and he found few friends in middle or high school. What kind of person would you expect to have emerged from that experience? If you met Josh, you would find someone who is loving, spontaneously fun, and insightful—you would be surprised that he endured such rejection and loneliness. While in college, Josh experienced the wonder of being welcomed, loved, and recognized for his gifts in a multiethnic Christian community at his school and also at an incredibly loving Asian American church. Today, he leads a multiethnic community made up of inner-city New Haven, Connecticut, residents and Yale PhD graduates—blacks, Asians, whites, and Latinos who trust each other across ethnic stories. Many submit to his gifted leadership and wisdom and are led to faith by his words and example. Though Josh grew up experiencing racism, bullying, and exclusion because he is black, his journey with Jesus transformed him into a leader of all people.

My husband, Shin, first encountered Josh's church after a season of being burnt out by ministry in his Korean American church and struggling to live up to his family's expectations. When Shin knelt to receive prayer at Josh's church, a handful of the pastors and ministry leaders laid hands on him. Those hands all belonged to black men, and Shin began to sob as he experienced, for the first time, healing from the hands of black American men. Shin grew up in a mostly black neighborhood in urban Plainfield, New Jersey. As a first grader, he had been the target of bullying and beatings every day during lunch and recess because he was the only nonblack kid at school. No one ever told Shin that not all black people are violent—it just so happened that these bullies were black (just as Josh's bullies all happened to be white). School administrators didn't know what to do, so they quarantined him with a teacher who would grade papers while he drew pictures. Shin learned to be afraid and avoided black American communities for the next twenty years, until spiritual emptiness and exhaustion led him to a multiethnic congregation. He didn't know that he needed healing in this area of his life.

"But God knew," Shin said as he recalled that moment where a hidden wall broke within him, "and these men became some of the closest friends in my next season of life. I learned about the beauty of the history of the black church, the pain my black friends go through, and about the poetry and artistry that flows from them like water." Shin could not have experienced this beauty and wept alongside his black sisters and brothers if he had not experienced healing in his perception and relationship with black women and men.

When our wounds are denied or ignored, further brokenness is caused. Try telling a person who was raped or abused that their pain was imagined, asked for, or "not really that bad." Depression, suicide, and other emotional problems can occur when such pain isn't validated. I've ministered to many college-age women and men who battle the depression and demons of such invalidation. When Jesus begins to redeem our ethnic identities, he doesn't deny the scars, pain, or sin that are in those histories. He says, "Let me in. Let me show you how you are made beautiful in the *imago Dei*, and let me heal the places of brokenness and sin."

HOW JESUS REDEEMS ETHNICITY

One of my favorite times of learning was during a team orientation for a short-term mission trip to Uganda in 2008. We heard from Lamin Sanneh, a Yale Divinity School missiologist who converted from Islam to Christianity as a teenager in Gambia. Sanneh held us spellbound as he spoke, and I remember his words as clear as day: "Every culture is like a water bay that anticipates the cargo of Christ. When Christ comes like a jet propeller plane and lands in that bay, he looks around and says, 'Look at the beautiful things in this bay. I made it this way. It bears the intended goodness of the Creator God.' Christ then looks at the places of brokenness, sin, and pain, and says, 'Let me excavate those places and fill them with myself.'" Jesus redeems our ethnic identities by affirming the created good in each of our cultures and by renewing, healing, and restoring the parts of our cultures that hold the effects of sin, brokenness, idolatry, and racism.

Richard Twiss, the late Native American theologian, writes about the importance of helping Native men and women embrace their ethnic heritage as good and asking Jesus to bring healing to their self-image as a Native person. This is a difficult task given the history of the church trying to rid the Native people of Native culture and language. Twiss shares the story of Bill, a Native man, who said, "When I started embracing the victory I have in Christ as being fully realized as a Native Christian, . . . I was empowered to become a whole person."[1] The beauty of Bill's ethnicity was amplified by Jesus, and the brokenness and sin were excavated and replaced with Jesus' healing, spirit, and truth. Twiss writes, "Jesus came to make our cultures better, not take them away from us."[2]

AMPLIFYING THE BEAUTY, EXCAVATING THE BROKEN

Jesus brings healing to our stories, not by denying them, but by addressing our wounds and teaching us to love even the unlovable parts. He brings affirmation of the good and healing in the broken in every part of our lives, including our ethnicities.

As Jesus redeems our ethnic stories, he shows us that we are made well. And he invites us to confess our places of sin, idolatry, lack of forgiveness, racism, and wounds. As we repent, surrender, and invite him to redefine our understandings of our ethnic selves, he brings healing, forgiveness, and restoration. This allows us to embrace the good we receive from the Creator God and to be healed.

My friend Dexter is Taiwanese American, and for most of his life, he bore the emotional, verbal, and physical abuse and brunt of his mother's dissatisfaction with her own life. When he became a

Christian late in college, he cried out to the Lord about the pain, silencing, hatred, and blows that his mother had aimed at him for most of his life. Dexter wrestled with the Scriptures that said honor your mother and father and love your enemies. He prayed for years that his non-Christian family would turn to Jesus. In the midst of this, Dexter heard a call to ministry, so he turned away from the affluence of working in finance. His parents cut off Dexter from the family, saying he had shamed them and that he was no longer their son. It was a painful and dark season. And still he prayed, sending flowers that were thrown in the garbage, his letters and emails unreturned.

Slowly, the Lord began to rebuild Dexter's relationship with his brother. After many years, Dexter started to see how God was using him to be a restorer and repairer of the family whose expectations and family idols had kept him trapped for so many years. When Dexter shares about his experiences of redemption with his family, many Asian Americans (but certainly also black Americans, Latinos, whites, and beyond) express a longing to see their own families restored, for parents to no longer be seen as oppressive gods but instead as the honored elders who point us to the goodness of God.

I met a Nadia, a young Latina woman, at a retreat and she told me about how she hated being Latina. Not only had she experienced racism aimed at her from white and non-Latino people, Nadia also repeatedly heard from other Latinos that she was "not Latina enough" because she didn't speak enough Spanish and had non-Latino friends. And she despised the machismo that led to misogyny and mistreatment of women in her family. "I don't fit here or there—my own people reject me. I have nowhere to go," she said. We spoke at length about what it meant for Nadia to forgive her own people and to forgive those that had rejected her, Latino and non. As she prayed forgiveness among her tears, she began to see herself as an ethnic Latina, a gift to those around her, and as someone who refused to participate in ethnic isolation even though everything around her told her to do so. Jesus was encouraging her to continue extending wide the *familia* embrace of God. He was both affirming the beautiful ways he had made her and also helping to remove obstacles that kept her from loving others in Jesus' name.

Jeremy is black and Nigerian American. Since his youth, he was teased and called a "Nigerian booty-scratcher" by other black children (also a common experience of many second generation African children). To hide his last name, he adopted the nickname "Jerry-O," which sounded cooler on the football field. He rejected associating with the ethnicity of his last name—which also held the painful reminder of a Nigerian father who had abandoned his family long ago. Quite unintentionally, Jeremy came to faith later at a Nigerian American church, and he became connected to his culture and ancestry in ways that he never could before. He learned to be proud of his name, proud of Nigerian songs and customs, and proud of the ways that God the Father made him as a Nigerian American and a black man. He also became a pastor and father figure to many high school youth at his black church who were growing up without knowing their fathers.

At the Urbana 15 Student Missions Conference, Native American participants sang "Holy Spirit Fiyah," a call and response song with improvisational dancing that represented their tribes of origin (both in dress and dance). They offered all of the beauty of their ancestral cultures to fifteen thousand people as an act of profound worship in a public, communal setting. Many people wept as they sang and watched these beautiful displays of uninhibited Native worship in tune with the *imago Dei* of Native cultures. It was as if the singers ushered us into one of the purest forms of worship, delighting in how the Creator God made us. A multiracial black woman who had recently been embracing her Native heritage texted me afterward, "I am weeping—why do the tears not stop?" I replied, "Because it is beautiful, and it is awakening a part of you that God placed there since the beginning."

I have the incredible privilege of working with an organization that has intentionally made space for helping Native students enter the kingdom without demanding that they shed their cultures or become "white" or "Western." And as Native men and women usher us into worship, I see greater openness from all to worship, lament, and listen to the Holy Spirit.

OUR NEW NAMES

When Jesus redeems our ethnic identities, he refuses to let us be defined by death and brokenness. As Jesus invites us into resurrection life, he renames us and calls us by what he is inviting us to become. He flips the lie of what we have been called or called ourselves on its head.

Instead of "slave" and "less than," Jesus calls black men and women to be prophets, leaders, queens, and kings in his name.

Instead of "unwanted foreigner" or "stranger," Jesus renames Latinas and Latinos as those who teach us the wide *familia* embrace of God so that all may know his name.

Instead of being defined by family scars and expectations, Jesus calls Asian and Asian American men and women to be restorers and repairers of our families and beyond.

Instead of "heathen" or "savage," Jesus honors Native women and men as the holy priestesses and priests of the living God.

Instead of "unwanted" or "terrorist," Jesus invites Middle Eastern men and women to be the most honored guests at the table.

Instead of "broken halves" of "incomplete wholes," Jesus tells multiracial women and men that they are fully white and fully Latino, fully Asian and fully black, fully Haitian and fully white. And they know better than anyone else how to navigate the complexity of multiple cultures.

But what about white women and men? What is the redeemed name that Jesus gives to white people, taking into account the history of privilege and racial tension with people of color in the United States?

I often see different mournful responses in white men and women who have chosen to engage in multiethnic community. One is the wistful, "Everyone has a culture but me. How do I regain what was never taught to me, or what my grandparents gave up because they were forced to assimilate?" The second is a deeper response to the reality of racial scars: it's a sense of shame for being white, for the history and legacy of racial injustice, for current inequalities and violence. Shame is different from guilt, as guilt is "I have done something wrong" while shame is "who I am is wrong." As a Southern white male friend mournfully asked after the shooting at a historically black church in Charleston, "What can save my people after so many centuries of blindness and injustice, sin and death?" What new name for white Americans will not ignore or disregard the historic pain endured by people of color?

A NEW NAME FOR WHITE BROTHERS AND SISTERS

A wise man once told me that you can judge a people by their proximity to their religious text. The Quakers were known for their commitment to scripture, prayer, and opposition to slavery. Levi Coffin, an American Quaker, was nicknamed the president of the Underground Railroad because of his lifelong work in the abolitionist movement during the early 1800s. Coffin helped between two and three thousand black Americans escape slavery and raised more than two hundred thousand dollars for the abolitionist cause. When Coffin was chastised by neighbors and friends for contributing to an illegal effort, he responded, "The Bible, in bidding us to feed the hungry and clothe the naked, said nothing about color, and I should try to follow out the teachings of that good book."[3]

As Coffin introduced his white community to the powerful narratives of black former slaves, they too became moved by the cruelty endured by these men and women. They too became convinced that slavery was incompatible with the gospel. Their homes became centers for making clothes for black escapees and part of the network of the Underground Railroad. Coffin and his fellow Quakers set up a fair-labor factory to sell slave-free goods and worked with a few white plantation owners who had freed their slaves and were paying them wages. He visited Canada to make sure that his black friends were safe and flourishing.

Coffin was influential and affluent, and he did not shy away from the reality that he was a white man with power and privilege. As is found in so many white stories, Coffin took individual risks and used that boldness for the good of others. He became a brother in arms with black men and women. He was not a white savior but instead fought alongside black people for a common cause. He became a freedom fighter.

In the spring of 2011, I was leading a spring break trip connecting service, justice, and faith as we helped rebuild parts of the Ninth Ward in New Orleans. Each evening, we discussed the relevance of Jesus to the conversation of justice in a room full of Christian and non-Christian students of varied ethnicity, including activist black students whose grandparents had ties to the South. One evening, I talked about white martyrs from the civil rights movement, many of them Christians, who had risked their safety, comfort, and lives for the cause of nonwhites. Many of the black students wept and asked, "I'm a junior in black studies . . . I'm a senior in urban policy . . . Why have I never heard these names?" In the midst of this emotional conversation, a black male student decided to follow Jesus. When I, an Asian American woman, shared the stories of white American Christians who chose to follow Jesus into sacrificial love at the cross and become reconciling freedom fighters, that example caused a black man to say yes to Jesus.

As I've taught on ethnicity and reconciliation that includes white people at the multiethnic table, I have become convinced that we often lack language or even a hope-based identity for how white Americans can engage in the conversation. The university has either shallow or retributive options for white people: ignore the scars or atone for their people's sins. It's easier to settle for a shame-based identity or self-atonement than dare to call white Christians to a hope-based identity that leads to deep sacrificial love and stewardship because we don't hear about white activists. We need to recover the stories of white Christians who helped the poor and oppressed, who fought for abolitionism, women's suffrage, and civil rights.

Instead of "oppressor" and "enslaver," Jesus calls white men and women to be freedom-fighters, advocates, and allies: sisters and brothers in arms who use their power and position to work alongside others to help restore the *imago Dei* in all.

CALLING FORMER ENEMIES BY A NEW NAME

But there's a problem with this story. We run the risk of forgetting the past if we choose to use a new name for a historic enemy of our people. How can I, as a Korean American, be reconciled to Japanese Americans after hundreds of years of injustice done to my people? How can black Americans (or Native or Latino) be reconciled to white Americans after slavery, genocide, and racism? Who pays the cost for this new name?

In the summer of 2008, I had the privilege of working with former child soldiers in Uganda. These young girls had been forced to kill their families and were kidnapped, raped, and birthed children. They had escaped from the bush with their young children but often ended up in villages where they had no male protectors and no trade skills to survive. The girls were targeted with violence because they were seen as the enemy. They represented the victim-turned-perpetrator, and usually the only groups helping them were faith-based, foreign nonprofits. The question lingered in my mind: Would they ever be accepted as part of the Northern Ugandan people?

After our time in Uganda, we traveled to Kigali, Rwanda. The Genocide Museum there is a sobering lesson about the depths of the depravity of the human heart. At the height of the affluence of Rwandan Hutus in 1994, they led a one-hundred-day genocide of 800,000 Tutsis and moderate Hutus, cutting down the Tutsi population by a tenth.[4] Tutsis and Hutus share the same ethnic history, but during the age of Belgian colonization, Rwandans with more European facial and cranial features were called Tutsi and given greater access to education, job opportunities, livestock, and housing. The remaining majority was called Hutu. The Tutsi-Hutu distinction would remain long after the Belgians left. And the enmity led to the 1994 genocide, with much government propaganda to support the destructive rage. Hutus turned in their Tutsi neighbors and families, which is why the Hutus were able to kill almost a million people in three months. When the dust of the genocide settled and the international community was in uproar over the atrocities, all the senior leaders stepped down. A young group of pastors and community leaders were tasked with leading the country out of its chaos.

The leaders formed the Truth and Justice Commission, but they quickly found their ability to administer justice was limited. Out of the remaining nine million Rwandans, over half were guilty of theft, rape, collusion, and murder. They did not have enough courts or judges to try the guilty, much less the prisons to hold them. They could execute those who were guilty, but was more bloodshed the answer? The larger problem was that the 1994 genocide was one of several in the cycle of ethnic cleansings that had reverberated throughout the past century.

The leaders needed to stop the hatred. One of the organizers, Antoine Rutayisire, told us, "The only way to put a stop to the cycle was to kill the hatred itself."[5] And the only way they knew how was through Jesus. So they renamed the Truth and Justice Commission to the Truth and Reconciliation Commission, because justice was not going to be possible. This was not a matter of distributive justice (redistribution of goods) or retributive justice (punishing the wrong). It was a matter of restorative justice—restoring the relationships that had long been broken in the hopes that such restoration would bring the long-term healing Rwanda needed.

Antoine spoke of how they adopted a Rwandan traditional justice process called *gacaca*, loosely translated as "justice among the grass," because the court meets outdoors. It brings together the entire village to hear from all parties involved in a crime, while respected elders serve as judges. For example, if someone stole a cow, the victim's family would say to the perpetrator's family: "Your son stole our cow and damaged us. Our relationship is broken." The perpetrator's family would respond, "Yes, our son did steal your cow, and we are so sorry for the damage it has caused you." After much dialogue and conversation, the perpetrator's family would say, "Here is your cow" (and offer another cow if they had the means) so that the relationship could be restored. They decided to apply this same reconciliation process to the victims and perpetrators of the genocide.

As Antoine explained *gacaca* to us, I asked, "I'm sorry, but are you saying that you asked someone whose mother and sister were raped and killed to forgive their enemy? That's a hard pill to swallow." Antoine solemnly raised his eyes to meet mine and said quietly, "Yes, we did. And they wanted to."

Many Tutsis wanted to forgive and be released from the burden of vengeance. Some Hutus were resorting to suicide after realizing that instead of being the heroes they had believed they would be (as was stated in the radio propaganda), they were internationally despised killers of innocent people. Christian Hutus confessed their sins and crimes, and Tutsis shared the pain and loss they suffered over many months. After many tears during the reconciliation meetings, they would rise, embrace, and go out into the streets of Kigali to talk about a day when Rwanda would no longer be defined by ethnic killing.

Antoine stretched his arms wide as he explained, "Only at the cross can victim and perpetrator die to themselves and rise as one new people."

Sin done to us and sin done by us has a cost we can't pay, and a power over us that we can't fight—without Jesus. God despises the desecration of his *imago Dei*, and he demands payment for such wrong. Death is the just sentence for a killer, an enslaver, or one who benefits from another's suffering. On a cosmic level, no amount of human effort can make up for the damage that is sustained in ethnic division, even though apology, reparations, and systemic changes are necessary on a human level. Jesus alone pays the cost for a new name. He pays the cost, the penalty for sinning against another and desecrating his *imago Dei*, when he dies upon the cross.

Not only does he pay this cost on the cross, but when he rises again, he breaks the power of sin in us. Corrie ten Boom, a Holocaust survivor, writes in *The Hiding Place* about meeting one of her captors at a German church after she spoke about God forgiving sins. He did not remember her, but she remembered him, and she froze as he extended his hand out to her and asked for her forgiveness. She did not want to. All the bitterness of her sister's death and the terror of the camp rushed back into her memory. But she needed to obey her Lord. She asked Jesus to help her as she struggled to lift her arm. And she felt a current, a healing warmth, jolt through her arm into their handshake, leading to the most intense experience of God's love she would ever encounter.[6]

Jesus gives us the power to forgive our enemies. He, as healer, has the power to bring healing to our broken concepts of our ethnic selves, to our idolatries and our divisions. God's death on a cross and his defiant reversal of death in the resurrection pays the cost and supplies the power to call an enemy brother and sister. There is no other space, philosophy, or religion that allows enemies to be reconciled as one people while fully acknowledging the wrong and fully committing to restoration.

"Only at the cross can victim and perpetrator die to themselves and rise as one new people." Antoine's words have reverberated through my soul and remain there, echoing. Only at the cross can privileged and oppressed die to themselves and rise as one new people.

WHEN REDEEMED ETHNIC STORIES HELP HEAL

In Ephesians 2:14-16, Paul writes, "For he himself is our peace, who has made the two groups one and has destroyed the barrier, the dividing wall of hostility. . . . His purpose was to create in himself one new humanity out of the two, thus making peace, and in one body to reconcile both of them to God through the cross, by which he put to death their hostility."

My college freshman year, a Japanese American minister stood before a group of mostly Korean and Chinese Americans and shared his horror at learning about the atrocities Japan committed against Korea, China, and many other Asian countries. He was full of sorrow but also full of quiet humility and dignity as he said, "On behalf of my people, I am so sorry for the violence, war, oppression, and injustice we committed against you." Many of us were stunned. Why would he do this? His family had lived in the United States for three generations and lived through the Japanese internment camps during World War II. He wasn't even born when Japan committed these acts! And yet, his words struck something in me as I realized that he was choosing to be someone different—a peacemaker and reconciler with those who had been oppressed by his people. His words of repentance exposed in me the unaddressed cracks in my ethnicity the sorrow and bitter anger I had never offered to Jesus. Jesus was not content with me defining my Korean American ethnic identity with disdain, bitterness, and distrust of an ethnic other. I could start to forgive without denying the scars of my people.

In the Rwandan reconciliation process, I found an answer for how Jesus redeems the ethnic stories of ethnic enemies and reconciles us to each other. He offers us the chance to die to our old selves and rise in the new. Jesus says to white Americans, "I made you well, and you are forgiven for what whiteness has meant in this country. Come and live a new story in me. Come and be a freedom fighter."

Over the past several years, I have had the opportunity to pray blessings over white men and women and to ask forgiveness for settling for an identity of shame for white people instead of an identity of hope. As black, Asian, Native, and Latino leaders of color pray over white sisters and brothers, their response is often shock, speechlessness, or weeping. One white person said, "I'm afraid to believe it because it sounds too good to be true." Another wept as he said, "Today was the first day that I sang the words 'people of every nation and tongue' and saw myself as one of them." A colleague said, "I knew that this was for real . . . because of the multiethnic group of people who prayed blessing and forgiveness. I don't know if there was any other way I could have understood that I was actually able to be redeemed as a white man."

It's amazing to watch these white men and women go back to their contexts and courageously engage in conversations about race, justice, and reconciliation. They look for people not being reached or served in their faith communities. They don't become courageous leaders by being ashamed of being white or trying to sound like a "hip" white person. They are called to be stewards of their ethnic identity, power, and privilege. They are more effective leaders and evangelists when they wield their white ethnic identities intentionally and humbly, instead of trying to ignore it, react defensively, or respond in shame.

THE HOPE AND RISK OF EMBRACING NEW NAMES FOR WHITE PEOPLE

It may be difficult for some, especially those who have suffered from unjust systems that benefited white people, to embrace a new name for white women and men. But just as Corrie ten Boom prayed in obedience, we must ask Jesus, "Please, help me to try."

I was leading worship during a season when the news told the death of an unarmed black person at the hands of police almost every other day. In a brief prayer, I acknowledged the pain in our country and the pain of our black brothers and sisters. After the service, I was accosted by an elderly white woman who was angry that I brought up race and accused me of dragging politics into worship, even though I had taken great care to avoid advocating for any political party during my prayer. She went on a long rant as I tried to engage her questions respectfully but firmly, but she seemed angry enough to hit me. Realizing that she wasn't interested in dialogue, I finally gently placed my hands on her shoulders and said quietly, "You are not my enemy. We might not agree on all things. But you are my sister in Christ." Looking taken aback, she paused and said that she would talk to the pastors leading the service about this instead. I cried later, at the shock of the encounter and the anger that came out of her lips. I prayed for her, even though much of me didn't want anything to do with her.

Many months later, I was surprised to see the woman at a prayer vigil for black men and police who had died in Baton Rouge, Philadelphia, and Dallas in the summer of 2016. She had gone from angrily colorblind to . . . open. During our previous encounter, she engaged me as an enemy and thought I would return the same. I wonder what would have happened if I had hit her back with my own words during that encounter. Would she have shown up to the vigil? I don't know if she and I will ever see eye-to-eye on all things, but Jesus may be turning her heart after all.

Daryl Davis is a black musician who decided to befriend members of the Ku Klux Klan after a chance encounter with a member at a club. He interviewed Klansmen, asking them the question, "How can you hate me when you don't know me?" Though Daryl is criticized for his methods by some, befriending the men led to trust-building between them, and Klansmen started handing over their robes to Daryl as a symbolic gesture. His friendship and engagement with Klansmen helped them see through the cracks in their reasoning into the common humanity that linked them both. More than two hundred men have left the Klan as the result.[7]

If we really believe what Paul writes, that Christ tore down the dividing wall between ethnic enemies, then we need to call white people to Jesus, God of hope. Instead of making white people feel bad for everything that was and is broken, we need to extend grace and forgiveness of the past. Then we can call them to the costly act of stewarding their whiteness for justice and mission.

OUR SCARS DEFINED BY HIS SCARS

In Luke 10:25-37, Jesus tells the story of a man attacked by robbers and left for dead who was helped by a Samaritan instead of his fellow Israelites. A Samaritan is the last person Jesus' audience would expect to defy the norms to help a stranger in need. By all rules that both Samaritans and Israelites lived by, he was not bound to help an Israelite, his ethnic enemy. And yet, the Samaritan risked his life on the winding roads from Jerusalem to Jericho as he moved slowly with a wounded man in full view of the robbers who awaited in the foothills; he paid several days' wages to an innkeeper to make sure that this stranger would survive.

Jesus isn't idolizing the Samaritan as better than the Israelites. He's describing a new kind of person—a new kind of humanity with a redeemed understanding of ethnic identity that can result when people choose to follow Jesus. The spiritual formation writer Joan Chittister says, "The Samaritan shows us that when I heal the other, I heal something in myself as well."[8] In binding the Israelite's wounds, the Samaritan was binding his own. What kind of scars and wounds would he have had to submit to Jesus, to pray and weep over, and to ask for healing before he could embody this counterculturally different way of being a Samaritan?

During a conference, I shared the story of a black woman living in South Africa during the time of apartheid who witnessed both her son and husband being burned alive by a white officer and his squadron. Years later, after the end of apartheid, the officer voluntarily confessed to these hate crimes in hopes of a lighter sentence. When the woman was asked about sentencing for the officer, she offered this reply: first, she wanted to visit where her husband was killed so that she could gather his ashes and bury him properly. Second, she wanted the white officer to visit her twice a month in the ghetto and to become her son, as she had no sons left. And third, she wanted the officer to know that he was forgiven because of the forgiveness she receives from Christ. As the woman walked over to embrace the officer, he fainted from the unexpected love and mercy in this "sentence."

At the same conference during a later time of prayer, a young Thai man said, "Buddhists killed my grandfather by burning him alive. I want to forgive them." I never would have imagined that there was someone at the conference who had lost a dear one through the same violent means. And yet the incredible story of mercy by the South African woman prompted the Thai man to also want to offer forgiveness. If one didn't believe that the cross and resurrection of Jesus was indeed the hope of salvation for the world, such stories would seem to be a mockery of ethnic pain, injustice, and sorrow. But our Lord calls us to obey him and love our enemies.

Forgiving our enemies is the stumbling block of Christianity, making the faith almost unpalatable to those who thirst for just vengeance. But we cannot pick and choose which commands Jesus calls us to follow. When we make the costly choice to obey Jesus because of the hope we have in him, it alarms and befuddles the secular world, where ethnic enemies are never forgivable. But we can't live as if Jesus wants us to forgive only those who look like us and share our ethnic experiences or only those who were similarly oppressed.

When we dare to consider forgiving our enemies, we are not saying that what they did was right or "not that bad." We are saying that what was done, particularly to our people, was so bad that the only thing powerful enough to eliminate the human need for vengeance and retaliation is the cross of Jesus. We can say to the great Judge, "I release my right to be the judge. I ask you to take this away from me."

Ethnic tension and racism affects every people group in the United States, in every country across the world. Miroslav Volf writes, "Forgiveness flounders because I exclude the enemy from the community of humans even as exclude I myself from the community of sinners."[9] Jesus wants to heal and restore all of us, and restore us to each other, in the *imago Dei* he intended. Will you let him?

QUESTIONS FOR INDIVIDUAL REFLECTION AND SMALL GROUP DISCUSSION

Make some space to prayerfully listen and ask Jesus to speak to you about the questions below.

1. What are lies or false names about your ethnicity or your people that he might want to remove?

2. Where is Jesus inviting you to forgive or be forgiven?

3. What is the new name that Jesus might be offering to you about your ethnic identity?

RECOMMENDED READING

Check All That Apply: Finding Wholeness as a Multiracial Person by Sundee Tucker Frazier

Exclusion and Embrace: A Theological Exploration of Identity, Otherness, and Reconciliation by Miroslav Volf

Following Jesus Without Dishonoring Your Parents by Jeanette Yep, Peter Cha, Susan Cho Van Riesen, Greg Jao, and Paul Tokunaga

The Heart of Racial Justice: How Soul Change Leads to Social Change by Brenda Salter McNeil and Rick Richardson

A Many Colored Kingdom: Multicultural Dynamics for Spiritual Formation by Elizabeth Conde-Frazier, S. Steve Kang, and Gary A. Parrett

Secure in God's Embrace: Living as the Father's Adopted Child by Ken Fong

Silence and Beauty: Hidden Faith Born of Suffering by Makoto Fujimura

InterVarsity Christian Fellowship has a *Beyond Colorblind* video series about ethnic identity. For a video about how Jesus brings redemption and healing to our ethnic identities, go here: http://2100 .intervarsity.org/resources/beyond-colorblind-redemption.

5

REDEEMED ETHNIC IDENTITIES SENT OUT TO HEAL

Paul grew up being aware of both his ethnic culture and the oppression his people had faced for centuries. From his earliest childhood days, he was taught to be proud of who he was and to value his people's culture and traditions.

Born Saul Paullus, Paul was a self-proclaimed Hebrew of Hebrews, from the tribe of Benjamin, circumcised on the eighth day, a Pharisee whose "righteousness based on the law [was] faultless" (Philippians 3:5-6). He was a symbol of the Jewish people's refusal to deny their heritage or view themselves as inferior amid the forced Hellenization imposed by Greeks and Romans. Rome was a multicultural empire whose ethnic diversity and tension mirrored our own world today. The empire grew through military conquest, oppression, and execution by crucifixion of anyone who opposed Roman rule, including many Jews.

Saul grew up in the ashes of such defeat and was part of a people who were struggling with what it meant to be a good Jewish person amid Rome-occupied Israel. The Pharisees emphasized Jewish laws of ritual piety, seeing holy living in everyday life as the best way of honoring the Torah in a troubled and changing world.[1] They were the popular and respected leaders among the people, and Saul learned from the best of them. The Pharisees firmly believed in resurrection, as did Saul. They saw Jesus' teachings as an affront and attack on their heritage and way of life, and they viewed Jesus' followers as traitors to their people. In ethnic, religious zeal, Saul led an all-out attack on Christ's followers:

> I persecuted the followers of this Way to their death, arresting both men and women and throwing them into prison, as the high priest and all the Council can themselves testify. I even obtained letters from them to their associates in Damascus, and went there to bring these people as prisoners to Jerusalem to be punished. (Acts 22:4-5)

It's on the road to Damascus that Saul is blinded by a bright light from heaven, as Jesus asks, "Saul, Saul, why do you persecute me?" (Acts 9:1-9). This leads to his conversion, the recovery of his sight, and a striking transformation in Saul, who starts to go by Paul.

Before his encounter with Christ, Paul represented a broken, oppressed people full of resentment toward every ethnicity that was not their own. But now his mission was to reach all, which meant crossing cultures, reconciling with ethnic enemies, caring for the poor, confronting injustice, and proclaiming Jesus as Lord. New life in Jesus brought healing to Paul's ethnic identity. Jesus took all of Paul's great knowledge and zeal for the Jewish Scriptures and turned that ethnic story into one that invited all into the kingdom of God. Instead of trying to destroy lives in order to preserve a broken human Jewishness, Paul was sent out to heal.

GLEAMS IN THE CRACKS

In Paul's life of mission, the beauty of Jesus' healing gleams in the former cracks of his ethnicity. Paul embraces his Jewish ethnic heritage and people and is committed to preaching to the Jews in his journey. His ethnic story is a canvas for telling Jesus' story to a broken world. As Jesus heals our cracks with his beauty, he makes us ready, individually and communally, to share his living water with others. We share his story of healing us with the world and call them to the same Healer.

When Brent, a black man who grew up in the church, got to college, he was heartbroken when his relationship with his girlfriend came crashing down. He contemplated taking his own life, and he realized that he needed Jesus' help to heal. Brent found a loving college fellowship where the campus minister, Andrew—a white man—insisted that there could be no gospel without racial reconciliation and multiethnic witness. Brent had grown up in the South, where he and his family endured many racist experiences. He was floored by the deep friendship, real conversation, and reconciliation embodied by Andrew and several other white student leaders. In experiencing real love and intentional community, Brent was able to forgive his enemies who had been white. He grew as a follower of Jesus and as a gifted leader and preacher.

Several months later, Brent, who was captain of the track team, was practicing on the field. A truck full of white men drove up and yelled threats at him and said, "What are you doing at our school, you f---ing [N-word]? Get out or we'll kill you."

Round and round they drove, yelling racial epithets and death threats. One of the guys stuck his head out the window and yelled his own name, as if he were challenging Brent to take action.

Afterward, Brent and his friends were angry and gathered to pray. The university administration heard about the incident and told Brent, "We will not tolerate people like that at our school. We will expel them and prosecute them. We don't need those people on our campus."

But Brent's gentle response shocked them when he said, "Those people? Don't you get it? You're one of *those* people. I'm one of *those* people. Don't act like they're some outside force. Because those guys were taught and encouraged to hate in their schools, churches, and maybe even on this campus. How can you say you want to educate when you don't want to embrace?" Brent told the administration, "If there should be a punishment, it should be forcing them to sit down with me over dinner to get to know me for the next several weeks." He refused to release the name of the student in the truck. When a CNN reporter asked why he was defending the assailant, Brent responded, "Because I love him. And you protect those you love." Brent was taking the call to love his enemies seriously.

Brent's witness powerfully called the campus to know the love of Jesus that is strong enough to break down racial walls. Brent, Andrew, and several other faithful women and men were willing to confront racial silence and colorblindness in their community. Their fellowship saw almost forty conversions happen in their group of eighty that year.

Brent's story has been used many times in sharing the gospel with non-Christians.[2] There is something powerful about it—about how he was loved by the ethnic other so that then he too could love his enemy—that brings people to repentance and healing. His story has helped white Southerners realize places of racism in their hearts; his story of loving the enemy has helped people of color realize where they have nursed hate for those who have wronged them. Jesus' story of healing gleams in the places of his scars.

PROCLAIMING THE KINGDOM
IN WORD AND DEED

We tend to think of Paul as the ideal evangelist and of his missionary endeavors being only about evangelism. But this does a disservice to Paul's story of reconciling mission. It reinforces a false belief that Christians should only care about spiritual salvation and personal piety.

Too often, evangelism and justice have been separated in the church. Evangelicals who emphasize personal piety and evangelism often regard social justice as a secular liberal agenda. But this is a false dichotomy! Matthew 6:33 reads, "Seek first his kingdom and his *righteousness*" (emphasis mine). Christians often assume this mean personal righteousness, with an emphasis on personal salvation. This reveals our own human bias. *Justice* and *righteousness* are translated from the same Greek word *dikaiosune*, showing that righteousness isn't just about personal pious living. It means both personal and corporate righteousness: personal piety as well as seeking justice for others. Martin Luther King Jr. writes, "Any religion that professes to be concerned about the souls of men and is not concerned about the slums that damn them, the economic conditions that strangle them and the social conditions that cripple them is a spiritually moribund religion awaiting burial."[3]

This doesn't mean Christians should pursue social justice at the expense of letting go of evangelism. But when Jesus said to "go and make disciples of all nations," he was talking about raising up Christ-followers who embody the kingdom of God in both word *and* deed. The hope found in Christ compels Christians to pursue justice and ethnic reconciliation alongside evangelism.

When Charlene, a black woman, walked into a meeting of Christian black students at the University of Virginia, she sat in the back of the room and thought, "I like you, but I don't like your Jesus." She wasn't religious and had been raised by her father, who told her, "You can be anything in college. Just not a Christian." But Charlene was outraged and hurting. Hate crimes and racist rhetoric had recently exploded on campus. The N-word had been scratched into the hood of her friend's car. Black students had been told, "Get off of our campus. You don't deserve to be here." So she was surprised when, after the prayer meeting, the group went out to peacefully protest what was happening on campus. Nonblack Christian students also joined them. Through their actions, Charlene saw that Jesus cared about ethnic injustice on campus. They told her that her black life mattered and was precious to God. Because Jesus followers engaged in combating racism and injustice, bathed in prayer, Charlene became a Christian.

Ethnic reconciliation is not separate from evangelism; it's not an extracurricular activity for Christians. When Jesus reaches out to the Samaritan woman at the well in John 4, he is doing reconciliation and evangelism at the same time. Jesus embodies a redeemed Jewish ethnic identity as he begins to challenge and heal the history of broken interactions with women, sinners, and Samaritans. As a Jewish man, he is sharing the story of God with non-Jews—the way it was always supposed to be. When the woman says yes to Jesus, she shares the good news with the village of her own people—a village she had avoided because of the shame of her broken past. Her ethnicity, and Jesus' ethnicity, no longer prevent mission. They become vehicles of mission.

STEWARDING OUR ETHNIC SELVES

When Jesus invites us into new life, he redefines all of who we are: our notions of manhood, womanhood, family, calling, purpose, histories, and ethnicities. Instead of throwing away our ethnicities, he calls us to steward them for kingdom purposes and use our power for good.

Jesus sanctifies power and shows us that our dominion is to help the flourishing of all. As we tap into Christ's resurrection power, we find strength to forgive, repent, pursue justice, lament, intercede, and advocate. We have the power to help the poor, love enemies, proclaim the kingdom, and to practice healing, restoration, and justice through lives of prayer and righteous obedience. As we anticipate the heavenly city and submit to Jesus as king, we are called to fundamentally challenge our broken notions of power, whether we are rich or poor, privileged or oppressed. We don't use power only for self-gain or only for our people but instead to care for others. Power for self-gain separates, but power used to love others unites without obliterating differences in personality, ethnicity, or gender. The church needs united, not uniform, witness.

The Evangelical Covenant Church (ECC) denomination started with Swedish immigrants to America in the 1800s. The heritage of its Swedish immigrants and commitment to mission are hallmarks of the ECC. As the denomination grew in size and wealth, they wanted to steward their resources for the sake of kingdom mission. Swedish Americans recognized their ethnic heritage and sought to help support the heritage of others. Connecting their story of immigration to the diverse churches around them, they chose to embrace Latino, black, Asian, and multiethnic congregations by offering training, fellowship, and spiritual and financial support. More than 20 percent of the ECC's congregations today are classified as ethnic (nonwhite, the largest being African American) or multiethnic. Recognizing that strength comes from diversity, the ECC now has a robust commitment to justice and missions overseas as well as church programs to engage racial reconciliation stateside. The ECC regularly assesses the authenticity of its ethnic ministry and diversity, including a commitment to share power, increasing ethnic participation in leadership, and sharing diverse stories.[4]

Mellody Hobson, an affluent investor who is black, gave a TED talk where she challenged listeners to have real conversations about race in order to pursue equal rights and opportunity in America.[5] She believes that instead of being colorblind, we have to be color brave. As an investor, she has seen that sound investments are best made with a diversity of people. In one example of color bravery, Hobson tells the story of John Skipper, a white Southerner who is the president of ESPN. He insists that every open position have a diverse pool of applicants. When asked, "Do you want me to hire the minority or the best person for the job?" he responds, "Yes." Hobson credits John Skipper's willingness to diversify as one reason for ESPN's success. Likewise, we as Christians can be better leaders, teachers, business leaders, and healthcare practitioners when we welcome diverse perspectives and learn from them.

My church was organizing a public forum on race and privilege with partnering churches and organizations. My white pastor, Dave—an accomplished speaker and the head of our large church-planting network—asked me to represent our church at the event instead of him. He said, "Our guest speaker is an older white guy, so if I'm also a speaker, we're just adding to the problem of white privilege that we're trying to address! We want your perspective as an Asian American woman who represents a good portion of our church." Dave was yielding the floor to me and trusting me, someone almost two decades his junior, because he knew that our community needed more than white and black male voices.

REDEEMED ETHNIC STORIES HELP PROCLAIM THE KINGDOM

We are called to steward who we are for good. When Jesus heals our ethnic identities, he uses that experience to better reach and serve those who look like us (our own people) and those who don't (those outside the village of our ethnic people). Many times, this means preaching and living out the gospel in ways that confront idols, ethnic barriers, racial scars, and unjust systems. But instead of this seeming like an impossibly difficult task, we should see it as a remarkable opportunity to share and live out the gospel.

A diverse array of more than one hundred Baltimore-area Inter-Varsity students gathered at a retreat about ethnic identity and the gospel. As we talked about how Jesus redeems our ethnic identities and calls us to care for those who are hurt on the side of the road like the Good Samaritan, the conversation and trust in each other deepened. People of every ethnicity invited Jesus into their ethnic stories and journeys. I had sweet dialogue with young white men who were grateful to reflect on their own stories and learn about others.

They said, "I really didn't know that things were still so bad. And I realize I can't be a true friend to my friends of color if I don't engage, don't try to learn, or don't speak up."

The retreat took place two months before the 2015 Baltimore protests in response to the death of Freddie Gray, a twenty-five-year-old black man who was taken into police custody and then sustained spinal injuries in a police van, slipped into a coma, and died days later. Tension between the neighborhood and the police boiled over and led to civil unrest. While many people pleaded for peaceful protest, others resorted to violence and destruction of property.

The InterVarsity student groups in Baltimore responded to the situation almost immediately by creating spaces of prayer and peaceful protest and by holding panels about race where students shared about their experiences and called people to follow Jesus. InterVarsity students also went to areas where the public schools were closed due to the unrest to help clean up, serve lunch to students, and care for the community. Judi, who oversees Baltimore's InterVarsity campus chapters, said, "I think it was God's timing that we talked about this at our retreat right before things blew up. There was no question whether we should respond, whether we should care." The compassionate actions of the InterVarsity groups got the attention of many non-Christians on campus. As more students were drawn to conversations about ethnic brokenness, they were surprised to hear that there was hope. Many students became part of a Christian community and started going to church to learn more about Jesus.

We must be willing to listen to each other's ethnic stories and truly love and view each other as sacred. In a world that prizes images on social media instead of real conversation and depth of relationship, the ethnically aware community can be a prophetic witness.

REDEEMED ETHNIC STORIES DEMONSTRATE
THAT CHRISTIANITY ISN'T WHITE

One of the challenges in sharing the gospel with people of color is the perception that Christianity is a white, Western religion. Many Asian Americans trying to share the gospel with family and friends hear that response. It's similar for those trying to share the gospel with black Americans who are suspicious of Christianity because of the ways it was used to justify slavery, and for Native Americans who see Christianity as a poison that destroyed their culture and people. Even white atheists and agnostics are suspicious of the muddled history of the white American church. Unfortunately, instead of having the gospel transform ethnic culture, the gospel was often conformed to cultural idolatries and prejudices.

But the gospel is not powerless against such brokenness. When we can both talk about the power of the gospel to bring healing between ethnic enemies and help someone live fully in their ethnic identity, Christianity becomes more credible. Jesus brings out the beauty of our cultures and brings healing into the best parts of our culture's ideals.

Julia is a Korean American woman. She loved her father, but they had a very complex relationship because he resented the primary role her Christian faith had in her life. One night, Julia's father asked her, "Who leads this household?" and she boldly answered "Jesus." Her answer caused so much anger in him that he repeatedly struck her. The pain from that event boiled over in Julia's life. As Julia and I prayed together about the incident, she asked Jesus to help her forgive her father, fully acknowledging that what he did was wrong but also realizing that her bitterness was carving her hollow. As Julia was praying, Jesus was there with her that night, covering her and holding back her father from hitting her. Afterward, Julia felt released from her numbing resentment.

Over time, Julia prayed for reconciliation with her father. Jesus began to show her how to honor and love her father, and they were able to reconnect. During one of their conversations, he unexpectedly asked for forgiveness for that terrible night. Jesus was transforming Julia's deepest wounds with her father, and when she shared that story with a close friend, that friend became a Christian. And because Jesus was leading Julia in honoring her father and forgiving him, her once antagonistic father was willing to listen to how Jesus was helping her to love him.

As Jesus restores us, and we live out that healing and share it, we have a powerful witness! As we share our faith and invite people to love God and love neighbor more deeply, we help turn people's attention to new places where Jesus can shape us into his image. We can encourage people to pursue lives of restoration, justice, and reconciliation. Evangelism doesn't need to be separate from the call to forgive others, reconcile, care for the poor, or stand up for the oppressed. In fact, evangelism that includes such stories makes the gospel even more compelling.

FAITH, HOPE, AND LOVE AS MOTIVATORS

It's one thing to be captivated by this picture. It's quite another to live it out day by day. Given the prevalence of everyday racial tension as well as the histories of our people groups, we don't know what will happen in conversations and interactions. Even our best attempts may end up causing pain to others or receiving pain from others. Shame, fear, and anxiety can often come up as a result.

A seminary professor once said to me, "God never uses fear, shame, or anxiety to motivate us." These are the unholy motivators, and Jesus does not use them to heal us, including our ethnicities. Fear (to be differentiated from reverence or fear of the Lord) is not how Jesus motivates his listeners. God doesn't motive us through shame (the sense that one is irreparably broken) or anxiety (the sense that one has not done enough). Shame, fear, and anxiety are used to uphold cultural idols and leak out in many of our conversations about race and ethnicity. But these are not God's motivators, and they can't be used to invite people to the kingdom.

Instead, God uses hope, faith, and love to invite us into his story and to heal our ethnic identities. Love is the fullest presence of trust, the antithesis of fear—for "perfect love drives out fear" (1 John 4:18). Instead of feeling shame about what we or our people have done or about what was done to us, we have hope in the power of the gospel to heal. Instead of anxiety about performing perfectly in multiethnic spaces and in growing in our ethnic identities, we have faith that God will lead us and provide the people, community, and experiences to help us grow in pursuing restoration.

Carol Dweck is known for her research on growth mindset psychology. She talks about the powerful impact of giving children a grade of "not yet" instead of Ds and Fs. Encouraging children to grow, and affirming their capability to grow, enabled elementary school students in underperforming inner city and Native reservation schools to outperform their peers. They stopped seeing themselves by their failing grades and realized they could be more.[6]

Likewise, we live in a world where we are defined by our earthly realities. We're told to bow to cultural idols, explicitly or silently taught to dismiss or hate certain people, or are the recipients of racism and prejudice. These deep scars make us either despise ourselves, our people, or other people. It makes us poor witnesses of the gospel, poor evangelists, and uncompassionate responders to ethnic pain and injustice.

In Jesus, we hold firm to what God sees when he looks at us. He sees what he made us to be, what he is calling us to be. Yes, we slip and fall, and we encounter incredibly difficult experiences of sin and brokenness, but Jesus says, "Remember who I made you to be, who I am healing you to be."

EXTENDING SHALOM WITH AN
INTERCESSIONAL "SORRY"

As you hear about the scars of others, sometimes you will represent the people who caused that person's wounds. The worst thing to do in that moment is to become defensive and try to excuse yourself or your people—because in doing so you're actually denying the person's pain. How can you extend shalom in such a space?

When you hear about ways Christians have hurt non-Christians, the proper response isn't to say, "I wish I weren't a Christian!" The response of sorrow and hope is to say, "On behalf of Christians, I'm so sorry for what was done or said to you. This doesn't reflect the heart of Jesus. Please forgive us." Without that apology, someone who was hurt by the church may not be willing to give Jesus a chance.

Stewarding your ethnic identity means owning your people, and acting as a reconciling representative of your people in extending shalom. When you hear about the way someone was hurt by your people, even if you don't know them, shalom is the best response.

My church, where the majority of attenders are people of color, went through a "Forgive Us" series where the pastors preached about ways the church had contributed to racism against minorities, sexism against women, hatred against the LGBTQ community, distrust of science, and more. Dave, a white pastor, listed ways the church had used the Bible to argue for support of slavery and the racist ideology of white superiority. On behalf of white Christians, he said, "I am so sorry." John, a biracial white and Korean pastor, listed ways the church and men had contributed to sexist and demeaning attitudes toward women. On behalf of Christian men, he said, "I am so sorry." When these men asked for forgiveness, some congregants were stunned while others wept. Many people of color said, "I have never heard a white man, a white pastor, so directly confront white supremacy and apologize before." Many women said, "I had never heard a male pastor apologize so specifically for pain caused to women."

This powerful experience spoke not just to the Christians but also to the non-Christians in attendance. Iranian and Chinese people were stunned to see leaders with power owning the sins of the past and asking for forgiveness. For them, such humility communicated something different about Christianity, compelling them to seek Jesus. It was beautiful to see them come closer to becoming Christians, and in the months after, we saw new believers and committed seekers say yes to following Christ.

Dave and John owned their people, be it white people, men, or Christians in general. They saw that it was important to do this if they wanted to extend shalom to those who had been hurt. This is an intercessional apology. Offering an intercessional apology goes a long way in building trust with people who have had ethnic tension with your people. You stand in the gap of the pain and offer shalom. In conversations about race, white people need to avoid the temptation to resort to the shame-based "we're terrible people" apology because it's actually a response of self-hatred and shame that's selfish rather than showing care for others. It's not a good witness.

For example, I'm aware that some Korean business owners take advantage of Latino and Southeast Asian immigrants. As a result, when I'm leading a conversation about ethnicity, I apologize in advance, saying something like, "On behalf of my people, I'm so sorry for the ways we hurt you. This was not what Jesus intended for your people or mine. Please forgive us. Could we work toward something new?" This intentional gesture helps build trust and the beginnings of reconciliation.

NEXT STEPS FOR STEWARDING OUR ETHNIC IDENTITIES

Jesus invites you to live your kingdom reality intentionally, in the vehicle of your ethnic identities. You're called to evangelism, reconciliation, justice, and a righteousness that declares the kingdom of

God to a broken world. Here are some ways to live out that kingdom mission.

Share your story as God heals you. The story of how God shapes and heals our ethnic identities is a powerful way to share the gospel. I've had conversations with friends and strangers, sharing about my own ethnic journey or the journey of others. Those conversations can quietly stir things in people, like letting light into a dusty room. People start to explore their own ethnic heritages. As God works in their stories, they then share with family and friends, who then also start to reflect on their ethnic heritage and stories. When you share the gospel with non-Christian friends, include the story of how Jesus is transforming your ethnic journey. Sharing your story invites both Christians and non-Christians into deeper healing with Jesus. Evangelism and discipleship deepen as a result.

Walk with those who are hurting around you. In order to understand how to pursue justice, we need to get close enough to the stories and experiences of suffering and injustice, just as the Good Samaritan did at the side of the road. Too often, churches care about the poor who live overseas while failing to address the needs of black and brown brothers and sisters that live nearby. We need to do both. Instead of trying to be "enlightened" people, we need to be compassionately aware people who are willing to address our pain and the pain of others. When Jesus heals our ethnicities, we don't need to fear the wounds we encounter. Jesus heals us so that we can step compassionately into those spaces. And when we can really listen to others, we are moved to compassion and action, to care for the poor, to offer friendship, and to speak up about unjust practices. If a racist incident happens on campus, at work, or in our neighborhoods, the worst thing to do is to pretend like nothing happened. The best thing to do is to show up, be present, hear their pain, and then pray and speak up together.

Continue to forgive as you proclaim the kingdom in word and deed.
Forgive, whether it be your ethnic enemy, a people who have harmed
you, or even your own people. I have met many Asian, white, Haitian,
Nigerian, and Latino women and men who have a hard time owning
their ethnic identity because of what their own people did to them or
their families. But if they do not own their people, they cannot extend
shalom on behalf of those people.

The more people you get to know outside of your ethnic experiences,
the more you will hear about the pain and injustice done to them. You
will likely feel the righteous anger of "This should not be!" But if you
leap into action without first asking Jesus to heal that anger, it can
become a destructive force. You may resort to shame, fear, and anxiety
to motivate action.

I regularly meet with white men and women like Stella, who was
looking for ways to help her white friends and family engage in conversations about race and ethnicity. She was frustrated and wrestling
with the injustices and blindness she saw in her own people. And she
was exhausted. I asked her, "Have you forgiven your people? For the
things that are wrong, the things they do and are deaf to?" She was a
little stunned and mumbled, "I don't think so." As we prayed together,
she saw that she was using shame to motivate those around her, often
with little success. But with a new understanding and a deeper commitment to racial reconciliation, she is now more able to engage
family and friends in conversation without resorting to frustration
and anger.

If you allow Jesus to help you forgive those who hurt you and your
loved ones, you stand a much greater chance at resisting injustice and
prophetically declaring Jesus' kingdom. Nonviolent resistance is the
prophetic act of loving your enemy while refusing to settle for the
world's standards. Nonviolent resistance was the foundational principle behind the civil rights movement. Protestors refused to fight evil
with evil.

Unredeemed ethnic identities will perpetuate unredeemed ethnic identities. Jesus calls us to be healed and to declare his kingdom in how we live out and steward our ethnic identities. As we become ethnicity aware, we need to learn how to live out the reality of that redemption. Ethnicity-aware behavior requires not just a mindset but the willingness to learn and embody the skills that help you build trust, learn others' stories, and share your story with Christians and non-Christians alike. It's essential to our witness and also how we care for each other and pursue justice.

QUESTIONS FOR INDIVIDUAL REFLECTION AND SMALL GROUP DISCUSSION

1. What is the story of Jesus' redemption of your ethnic identity that you might want to share with non-Christian friends? What is compelling about your story?

2. Who might Jesus be calling you to reach out to with the story of his healing in your ethnicity?

3. Where might Jesus be calling you to show up, listen, and pursue justice?

4. Where might Jesus be calling you to forgive an ethnic enemy or your own people?

5. In learning about ethnic identity and race, where have you experienced fear, shame, or anxiety or used it with others? Where is God calling you to use hope, love, and faith as motivators instead?

RECOMMENDED READING

A Credible Witness: Reflections on Power, Evangelism and Race by Brenda Salter McNeil

Forgiving as We've Been Forgiven: Community Practices for Making Peace by L. Gregory Jones and Célestin Musekura

Living Gently in a Violent World: The Prophetic Witness of Weakness by Stanley Hauerwas and Jean Vanier

Living Without Enemies: Being Present in the Midst of Violence by Samuel
   Wells and Marcia A. Owen

InterVarsity Christian Fellowship has a *Beyond Colorblind* video
series about ethnic identity. For a video about how Jesus sends us out
to heal in our ethnic identities, go here: http://2100.intervarsity.org
/resources/beyond-colorblind-restoration.

PART
TWO

STEWARDING
OUR ETHNIC
IDENTITIES

6

TRUST-BUILDING
WITH ETHNIC
STRANGERS

Daniel is a quiet, lanky Chinese American man. While ministering at a local college, he would ask the students he mentored, "Where are you going next?" If it was appropriate, he would ask, "Would you take me with you?" Then he would strike up spiritual conversations with his students' friends, which helped his students observe trust-building ways to communicate. Daniel was eager to hear people's spiritual questions, and he asked how he could be caring for and praying for the different communities he encountered. Daniel's calm and easy-going demeanor easily won the trust of the strangers he met.

One day, he went to the Black Student Union (BSU) with Shauna, one of the black women in his group. Clearly, he was not black, but he was warmly greeted by Shauna's friends. Suddenly, a stern-faced young Jamaican American man walked up to Daniel and asked, almost demandingly, "What are *you* doing here?" Daniel was quite taken aback, but he responded, "I came with Shauna to meet BSU students and ask about how I could be praying for you and how our community could better serve you spiritually." The young man's demeanor softened and he said, "That's cool." Daniel and the young man then started a conversation together that was quite different in tone to the original question.

"What are you doing here?" was probably the question reverberating through the Samaritan woman's head when she first met Jesus by the well in John 4. Jesus does the unexpected thing by asking her to give him a drink. She responds with, "You are a Jew and I am a Samaritan woman. How can you ask me for a drink?" (John 4:9).

Now when some of us read that, we think, *Come on, lady! It's Jesus, for crying out loud. And he's not doing anything terrible—just asking for a drink!* But we must remember the context. Jesus was a Jewish man traveling through the heart of Samaritan territory. Six hundred years of ethnic tension, civil war, and bloodshed divided their peoples. When this Samaritan woman sees Jesus, she sees his ethnicity. Was this going to be an aloof, condescending, or hostile Jew? The last thing she expects is kindness.

WHAT DO THEY SEE WHEN THEY SEE YOU?

We learn a lot about Jesus by looking at what he does to build trust with this Samaritan woman, who doesn't know the good news and has every reason to distrust him. Jesus wants to share his good news with her, but he needs her to trust him in order for her to be able to hear it. In their book *I Once Was Lost*, Doug Schaupp and Don Everts write that trust-building is essential in connecting with a non-Christian so that they can eventually get to a place of spiritual conversation.[1] Without trust, you can't move forward in sharing the gospel relationally.

Likewise, we can't just share the story of Jesus and his redemption of us in our first conversation with someone. Talk about intense and potentially scary. Jesus could have said to the Samaritan woman, "I'm a nice Jewish man, I promise!" But that may have further raised the woman's suspicions and possibly led to the question, "Do you even know how to be kind to me?"

Imagine you're a Kintsukuroi cup that has been resealed to show the gleaming story of Jesus' healing in you. Someone places you in a cupboard with other cups and vases, many with cracks. While Jesus' story in you is beautiful, *the way you interact with others matters*. Happily proclaiming your redemption story while bumping into the other cups will cause their cracked parts to deepen. Your carelessness doesn't communicate the gospel to the other who needs Jesus' redemption and healing. We need skills to live in multiethnic community.

Many of us enter into ethnically diverse communities and church settings with good intentions, wanting to communicate that we are not one of "those people." But words without countercultural actions are cheap. We need show that we are trustworthy by understanding that when we interact with an ethnic other, we could represent any of the following *and have no idea which one we are*:

1. A person whose people have been friendly with their people
2. A person whose people have been hurt by their people
3. A person whose people have hurt their people
4. A person whose people have avoided or remained distant from their people

You can hope that you're a category one person to all people, but that's not likely in our broken world. So how do you start reconciliation with someone who may or may not like you because of your ethnic background? The solution is not to be colorblind. The solution is to start by building trust.

Ethnicity-aware trust-building is essential to inviting people to Jesus's table. Many non-Christians don't know that Jesus is good news, much like the Samaritan woman who regarded Jesus with suspicion. The small ways we enter into conversation lay down the foundations of trust for long-term relationship as we embody God's hospitality to believers and nonbelievers alike.

We must offer the hospitality of God to a racially and ethnically broken world by adopting and embodying crosscultural skills. Jesus did such when he stopped by the well and asked the Samaritan woman for a drink. He asks for a favor and addresses her as "woman" (the Greek text uses the word *gynai*, which some modern English versions of the Bible translate as "mother").[2] Even so, the woman was suspicious that a Jewish man would even try to talk to her. But that request started the slow process of her asking questions, seeking, and entering the kingdom. Likewise, we need to first intentionally build trust across ethnicities and cultures.

GREET THE SAMARITAN WOMAN

The very first step is a simple one. Jesus travels to the middle of Samaria to greet a woman ethnically different from him. Likewise, do the same: go and visit a community that is ethnically different from yours, entering in with a learning posture.

When Tina, a Korean American, realized that a large Vietnamese community on campus wasn't being reached, she didn't invite them to her Christian group. Instead, she befriended some Vietnamese students, which led to visiting the Vietnamese Student Association and attending their meetings. She built trust by learning their culture and stories, which eventually led to spiritual conversations and conversion.

My friends who work at urban, mostly black community centers have a common refrain they share with potential volunteers: don't be like all the other suburban, mostly white volunteers that come in and try to "fix" everything. If you don't have trust with the people in the room, your suggestions will sound condescending, uninformed, or just plain prejudiced. Participate by listening and observing. The volunteers that thrive are the ones who come in quietly and serve while learning. They earn the respect and trust of the community's gatekeepers, the people with influence who say, "This guy is trustworthy. He's with me."

Conversely, when someone steps into your space—church, school, or workplace—and is the ethnic minority in the room, extend hospitality. Be the first to say hi and welcome them. I do this with white, black, and Latino newcomers at my majority Asian American church. I've been surprised at how willing ethnic minorities have been to stay at our church, but they tell me, "You and your husband made us feel so welcome. It helped us decide to make this our home." Invite your coworker out to lunch, say hi to your neighbor or dormmate. Being the minority due to ethnicity, gender, class, field of study, life stage, or profession can always be an isolating experience. Counter that and be someone who embodies Jesus, who sees each and every person.

What you're not doing is asking someone to be your token "special friend of _____ ethnicity." If you're white and extending hospitality toward a black American, you are choosing to extend Jesus' hospitality in a countercultural way that challenges the historic enmities between the two. If you're Asian American and extending hospitality toward a Latino American, you are counterculturally challenging the lack of positive meaningful interaction between those people groups. When Jesus greets the Samaritan woman and chooses to have prolonged dialogue with her, he is honoring her in ways that were unusual for his people. Go out of your way to greet people who don't look like you.

ACKNOWLEDGE ETHNICITY BY ASKING ABOUT ETHNIC BACKGROUND

In the rhythm of get-to-know-you questions, Asian Americans (like many other people of color) almost always get asked a question about their ethnic background. However, it's almost always poorly worded, as in,

"Where are you from?"
"Where are you *really* from?"
"What are you?"

For some African and Caribbean American children of immigrant families, they can answer the question of "Where are you from?" with pride, displaying their strong connection to their motherland. However, for most people of color, "Where are you from?" is implicit code for "I'm asking where you are from because you obviously don't belong here." It becomes a painful question that excludes because it assumes that white is the norm, or that only white and black people are Americans. Often, the person asking the question never intends to cause the kind of dissonance, pain, or anger that comes up, though it does reveal their bias. Think of asking that question of someone who is adopted. Do we really want to ask someone who is aware that they grew up away from their biological parents, "No, where are you *really* from?"

Some people of color, particularly biracial or multiracial people, get asked, "*What* are you?" as if people can't easily categorize them and so ask out of consternation or confusion. But such a question and tone are inhospitable. They treat a person like an animal or a thing to be categorized instead of a person.

What's the alternative? In the get-to-know-you process of asking questions, I start with something simple to find some common points of connection, such as, "What do you do?" or "How long have you lived here?" Then I ask, "What's your ethnic background?"—and I ask this question of everyone, including white people.

When I asked Tiernan, a tall, platinum-blonde, blue-eyed woman, "What's your ethnic background?" she raised her eyebrows and chuckled as she said, "Well, clearly I'm white." I responded, "Yes, but you have the name of a Viking lord. Who named you? What's your ethnic background?" It turns out Tiernan (a woman's name that's Gaelic in origin) has German and British roots, including a little bit of Irish. Then, just as I would any other student of color, I asked when her ancestors came to the United States and what she knew about her extended family, which resulted in a fun conversation. By asking this question of every person, even white people, it validates that we *all* have an ethnicity.

"What's your ethnic background?" is a great way of asking someone about their ethnicity, and it avoids the less tactful and offensive alternatives. You might want to try out some other variants that feel more natural to you, such as, "What's your family's cultural background?" or "Tell me about your ethnic heritage." A good follow-up question is, "Where's home for you?" You can learn about the part of the country or the world people grew up in, and those who were constantly transplanted can answer open-endedly.

A question such as "What's your ethnic background?" allows for a bigger answer than asking the more limited, "Where are you from?" It gives space to responders who are mixed, adopted, identify with their international roots, and more. For example, instead of assuming that someone is Chinese, the question allows someone to identify as Cambodian American. Instead of assuming that all Latinos are Mexican, it allows someone to identify as Salvadorian. Instead of assuming that all Native Americans are the same, "What's your ethnic background?" allows someone the space to explain their place in the tribal diversity of the Native American people. In an increasingly more multiracial and diverse America, we need this question.

Not all people who are multiracial *look* multiracial. A light-skinned person of African descent could be the child of multiracial parents, or two light-skinned African Americans, or black Caribbean (Afro-Latino) parents. Instead of trying to guess, it's better to ask and learn about their beautiful complexity.

As you ask more people, "What is your ethnic background?" you're going to become more aware of the differences and similarities within macro-ethnic groups: white, black, Asian, Latino, and more. After you ask about hundred people in each macro-ethnic category about their ethnic backgrounds, you'll start to notice the differences between Southern and Western Europeans, Korean Americans versus Vietnamese Americans, Indian Americans versus Middle Eastern Americans, Puerto Ricans versus Dominicans, Haitians versus Nigerians versus black Americans descended from slavery.

However, this should not be the first question you ask someone! Get to know their name, what they do for work or what they're studying, where home is for them. Ask about ethnic background once you get past some of the niceties of small talk. After multiple interactions, you could ask, "What's it like being (insert ethnicity) at your church/school/workplace?" This is a deep question that asks them to share their genuine experience, so don't ask if you're not willing to listen and refrain from arguing with the person. They may share things that are new to you.

ASK GOOD LEARNING-POSTURE QUESTIONS

We need to ask good questions that communicate our genuine interest in learning more about others' ethnic backgrounds and cultures. People almost always feel more engaged if you ask them to share versus trying to prove how much you know about their ethnic background.

What makes a good question? Make sure that the person receiving your question doesn't feel like they have to defend who they are in answering your question. Don't make them feel like they are in a courtroom or a laboratory. Interrogative or accusatory questions make it sound like the person is different from *your* assumed normal and often make the person feel unsafe.

Here are some examples of questions and statements to avoid:

- "Why do you do that?"
- "Why do your people or _____ people do that?"
- "That food/event/experience was _____ (gross, inefficient, chaotic). Why is it like that?"
- "Aren't you just overreacting? Why did you say that?"

For example, you may come from a culture where eating animal organs (tripe, liver, stomach) is not normative. However, most cultures around the world do eat all parts of the animal. If you say, "Ew, that's gross," what you end up saying is, "Your food is not normal, your people are not normal." You define normalcy by your own standards, which ends up alienating people by making them feel uncomfortable.

Now, on the other hand, you may come from a culture where eating fermented milk solids developed by bacteria sounds terrible. But—surprise!—this is how cheese is made, which is normative to some and not to others. Everyone has a different reference point of what is normal, and we should stop asking questions that sound like we're wondering why the person is not more like us.

In general, we need to avoid accusatory questions. Instead of putting the person on the spot for not being like you (with you as the judge and jury), it's helpful to choose clarifying questions that invite deeper sharing. Start off by stating your desire to have good relationship with the person by asking a clarifying question.

- "Could you tell me more? I'd love to understand better what that experience was like for you."
- "I think I missed something back there. Could you help me understand what was happening when ____ happened?"
- "Forgive my ignorance, but I don't know what ____ is. Could you explain it a little more so I can learn? Or is there a book I can read to learn more?"
- "You seem upset. May I ask what is going on for you?"
- "This might be an uncomfortable topic, but at some point, I'd love to know about what this is like for you. Could we talk about it sometime when you feel comfortable?"

These kinds of questions put you in the seat of responsibility, allowing you to embody a humble learning posture so that the person being asked doesn't feel defensive.

One day, Walt, Julian, and I were walking together out of a seminary class. Walt is white with Irish American roots; Julian is black, born and raised in Chicago. Walt is a laid-back and thoughtful sports guy; Julian is an Ivy League graduate who loves jazz and Nietzsche. They both love theology. Walt asked us how we liked the class. I responded that I really appreciated the professor's wide range of historical knowledge but noted that most of his stories about his diverse church congregation involved internationals, not American people of color. Julian mentioned that he found some things helpful, but he really struggled to receive the teaching because the professor was a middle-aged white man that reminded him of several white male pastors that in the past had hurt him and his mother, a black Methodist pastor. He also found some of the professor's anecdotes pretty unhelpful.

Walt, a white man, had a choice. He could have just politely nodded and changed the topic, or he could have asked more questions. Walt bravely chose the latter and asked Julian, "Could you tell me a little more about what you found hard to receive from him as a professor? I'd love to understand more."

Walt was training to be a pastor, and I was proud of him for asking a question instead of staying silent. Julian opened up, and Walt listened with compassion and respect as Julian shared about how his black family's experiences with police differed greatly from the white professor's. As we continued to talk, Walt and Julian started to bond over their mutual appreciation of theology, and it was wonderful to see them get to know each other on a deeper level. Walt's learning posture helped communicate safety and friendship across the history of Julian's bad experiences.

AVOID GENERALIZING

Learning about different ethnic backgrounds will help you build a base of knowledge and stories that helps you connect the dots. As you ask people about their stories, avoid language that generalizes or makes assumptions of others. Not everyone that is black will speak a certain way. Not everyone that is Asian or Asian American will have a certain type of personality. No one story will be the same for all Latino Americans. Not all white Americans are affluent.

In the movie *The Namesake*, the main character, Gogol, is an Indian American trying to fit in with his fellow New Yorkers. When he meets his girlfriend's family friend, a white woman, she goes on a droning monologue about what she knows about India. It's uncomfortable, and he doesn't really have anything to say other than to politely nod. In my own life, I don't feel connected to someone who tells me, "I visited Korea once," or "I have a Korean friend." That's about them trying to show they're enlightened, not about actually getting to know me.

Instead of such shallow attempts at conversation, become a story gatherer, someone who is quick to ask other people about their experiences. If you ever find yourself in the dangerous mindset of thinking or telling someone that you know more about their ethnic experience than they do, it's time to check your pride and assumptions.

In the story of the Samaritan woman at the well, she tries to distance herself from Jesus when she says, "Our ancestors worshiped on this mountain, but you Jews claim that the place where we must worship is in Jerusalem" (John 4:20). Little does she know that her generalization of Jews does not fit *this* Jewish man.

In starting conversations, avoid assumptions about wealth, poverty, or preference for worship. You might start to notice some patterns or trends about these things in the stories shared by, for example, your black or Asian friends. Then it's okay to ask them, "I think I see a pattern in the stories that you, Shelly, and Kyle tell. Is this a cultural thing, or do you just have some uncanny similarities?" Let your friends correct or affirm your observations.

My friend Andre, who's black, had painful crosscultural conflict with a Chinese American coworker. Andre values passion, immediate responses, and engaging in conflict. He felt that his Chinese American colleague was reserved, careful, and almost too cerebral, which made Andre come to the conclusion that his colleague didn't care about the team and its mission. Andre said to me, "It's so weird because I grew up around Asian people." I responded, "You grew up around *Korean people*. That's a huge difference." Andre was expecting his colleague to act Korean and so was misinterpreting his colleague's quiet, more reflective nature as indifference.

As I meet more people, I see the influence of regional culture as well as ethnic culture. To me, the feel of white, black, Asian, and Latino folks from the Northeast is markedly different than the same ethnic counterparts from California, Texas, the South, or the Midwest. My Southern black friends are friendlier than my more reserved New England black friends. My white friends from Boston are more formal than laid-back Southern Californian white folks. My Jersey Asian friends are sassier than their Midwestern counterparts.

AVOID OFFENSIVE LANGUAGE
AND STEREOTYPES

Regardless of regional differences, it's important to know what trigger points to avoid. One of these in particular is ethnic slurs. It's *never* okay to use ethnic slurs to refer to any ethnicity.[3] I list some in the endnotes just so you know what I'm talking about. *Never* say these in conversation, perhaps with the exception of relaying a painful experience that happened to you. They reinforce derogatory stereotypes of brothers and sisters of our community, including white Americans. If you are not aware of what other ethnic slurs you need to avoid, search the internet for "derogatory ethnic slurs." Any time I use a video clip or a testimony in my teaching that includes a slur word (particularly if it's the N-word), I explain that we are not to repeat the slur because it inflicts pain.

There is debate about the N-word. Some rappers and black folks use it in different scenarios, so some nonblack people wonder why they can't use it. There are also nonblack people who are told by their black friends that it's okay to use the N-word. My response is this: black Americans themselves differ widely on this issue, and more importantly, we choose not to use the N-word because we want to be ethnically aware and invite others to Jesus and deeper community. Paul says to avoid every kind of evil (1 Thessalonians 5:22). Every ethnic slur has a history of pain, and so it's better and more loving to avoid it when you know that it could trigger pain for others. What do you have to lose by being more hospitable and intentional? Choose to proactively love by avoiding a potentially hurtful word.

Different ethnic groups have some sensitive trigger points that you want to avoid. For example, Asian Americans are often called *exotic*, but such labels often betray an opinion that Asians are foreign and therefore un-American. That adjective has historically been used by Westerners to dehumanize Asian women into sexual objects. Black women despise having their hair touched by random strangers who don't ask for permission and then exclaim, "It's so different!" (This is similar to when people touch the belly of a pregnant woman without asking.) It's a kind of exoticism that makes black women feel like objects at a freak show instead of people whose beauty should be genuinely admired.

I could make a long list of what not to do, but the general principle is to be aware of the larger historical scars that affect different ethnic groups. They will give you a clue as to the trigger points for different people groups because trigger points connect to larger historical contexts. Black men and women were treated as slaves, chattel, and seen as less than and not as real American people. Comments that express surprise about a black person being "articulate" betrays a bias about the intelligence of black people. Historically, Asian Americans were seen as exotic foreigners. When they are told, "Your English is really good," such a comment reinforces the painful experiences of being treated as un-American. Because Latinos are viewed as unwanted "illegals," neglecting to welcome and include them is painful.

White people also have some trigger areas, including a strong reaction to the words "white privilege" or "white supremacy" because they don't really understand what those words mean. They often hear those words as an attack on them personally instead of hearing them as descriptions of historical and current practices of injustice. Combined with bad previous experiences in conversations about race as well as the dogged fear and desire to prove that "I am not a racist!" dialogue with white people can get very difficult. I've found that if I explain the larger meaning of those words, white people are more able to enter into conversation. This also allows me to be sensitive to lower-income white Americans who don't resonate with having power; they struggle to understand that they do have privilege. My interest is not that they agree with the terms as labels—I want white people to understand the larger realities and steward their ethnic identities in those spaces.

Another general principle is to ask your friends whose ethnicities differ from yours about some unhelpful or offensive things that people do or say to them. You can also look it up on the web or read a book about the topic. But because you and I live in different places, I can't presume to understand the regional context of where you live. Your friends of various ethnicities in your sphere will be some of the best teachers of what to avoid and what is acceptable. But you need to be willing to ask and learn.

EMBODY A LEARNING POSTURE AND INVITE OTHERS INTO THE SAME

If your friends point things out to you and correct you, receive that teaching. When you're in a multiethnic community, you should always be learning about new experiences and new people, going to new depths. You're never going to arrive at some destination of expert knowledge; instead, you're in for a lifetime of learning. It's not about learning the answers to a test. It's about learning the steps to a dance so that you can enjoy the music and build on old steps as you encounter new moves and rhythms.

Every crosscultural experience with a new person or an old friend has potential to be a place of dissonance. If you make a mistake or encounter tension and then choose fear, anxiety, suspicion, or self-protection, you will end up responding by withdrawing, leveling criticism or accusation, and breaking trust in relationships. Choosing to be a learner means approaching with openness, adaptability, and curiosity. The end results will be deeper understanding and empathy in relationships.

As you grow in being part of a multiethnic community, you will find yourself in the position of being both learner and teacher. Have grace for yourself as you learn and make mistakes. Be quick to apologize and ask for forgiveness, and make sure you understand what you need to change. If you're not sure about the outcome of an interaction, ask the person or someone who observed the interaction.

I had a bad habit of half-sitting and leaning on furniture that wasn't designed for sitting. When visiting my friend Jeannie and her mom, I started to lower my butt to sit on an ornate dresser, not realizing that I was about to majestically plant myself on Grandma Chu's ashes. Jeannie and her mom looked horrified and stopped me by yelling, "No!" I was thoroughly embarrassed, but I apologized profusely and asked for forgiveness. They were very gracious, and we were able to laugh about it afterward.

Likewise, when you see someone making mistakes in crosscultural interaction, be gracious toward them and help them learn how to be a better member of a multiethnic community. Avoid the accusatory confrontation of, "Why did you do that? Don't you know better?" Oftentimes, the person does *not* know better. Coach them on how it could be better next time. Don't focus only on what they did wrong—focus on what is being missed and the kind of interactions and friendships they could have in a multiethnic community.

I was part of a small group in which one of the women had never had friends of color. Linda was a white Southerner. She was easy to like, but I immediately noticed that she would say offensive comments without realizing that they were offensive (like calling sushi "gross"—my Asian sensibilities were deeply offended).

One day, we were by a lake and saw a flock of ducks. Seeing a duck with a darker, spotted complexion, Linda commented on how it was ugly. Her next comment unnerved me: "It's an African American duck!" Linda didn't seem to notice that her two comments were connected. I stood there wrestling with whether or not I should say something to her. I had just met Linda days earlier, and I didn't want to shame her. But better me than a black friend who would have to endure such a conversation.

I talked to Linda the next day, and I said that while I enjoyed her company, I had something uncomfortable to bring up with her. I asked her to recall the conversation by the lake about the ducks. She said, "I said the duck was ugly and then . . ." Her eyes opened wide and she clapped her hands over her mouth. "I said it was an African American duck! Oh no!" Linda had not realized what she had said or the negative impact of those back-to-back statements until we replayed the conversation. Gently, I told her that some of her passing comments were not indicative of the warm and welcoming person I had experienced her to be otherwise. Weeks later, Linda sent me a card, thanking me for having a real conversation with her in a loving and gracious manner. She said it had opened her eyes to so much more around her. She wouldn't have known if someone had not confronted her, and she would have repeated the same mistakes. Now, Linda could be more aware and sensitive to what she thought and spoke. She grew into a stronger and more effective leader as a result.

ACTIVELY ADDRESS YOUR IMPLICIT BIAS

Andrew was a junior and serving as a residential advisor; his friend Daryl was the only black advisor among the twenty or so residential advisors. One day, one of their friends asked them if they remembered the classic '80s movie *The Breakfast Club*. Most of them said yes, but Daryl's response was surprising: "I hate that movie."

"Why do you hate it?" Andrew asked him later. Daryl responded, "Because no one in it looks like someone I can relate to. Everyone is white."

Andrew said he felt like scales fell off of his eyes. Daryl was right—every character in the movie was white. And if Daryl felt that way about this one movie, then what other life experiences would feel similar for Daryl and other black or nonwhite folks?

Andrew realized that he had falsely assumed that his ethnic experience was "normal." I catch many white and nonwhite Americans referring to a white person as "American," as if *white* American is the assumed normal (I often correct them by saying, "You mean '*white* American'").

Nicolaus Copernicus was a Renaissance-era astronomer and mathematician who blew everyone's minds when he said that the sun, not the earth, was the center of our solar system. We need a Copernican revolution in how we think of ourselves in multiethnic community—our ethnic cultures are not at the center! The only thing that serves as our center is Jesus, who helps us identify our idols, cultural beauty, and biases.

If you have grown up in the ethnic majority or around people who are ethnically similar to you, you may view yourselves as "normal" and others as "abnormal," particularly if you are white and from a majority white context. Let go of the mindset that your normal is the right normal. In America, whether you are Asian, Middle Eastern, Latino, black, or white, we are all American. Canada, England, France, South Africa, Brazil—people of every ethnicity call those countries home. Our ethnic backgrounds enrich how we live out our nationalities. We should stop referring to white people as American and others as not.

Each of our cultures have sayings and assumptions about who are "safe" and "good" people and who are "bad" and "unsafe." Our media is dominated by mostly white-normative views of ethnicity, so black people are often characterized as loud, emotionally volatile, violent, and criminal. Asian Americans are thought to be quiet, submissive, weak, and effeminate. Latinos are characterized as lazy or dangerous,

Middle-Easterners as Muslim and terrorist, Native Americans as nonexistent or exotically "other." White people are seen as less violent and more upstanding citizens, and this is seen in how we respond to strangers we encounter in the street. A study by Keith Payne shows that both white and nonwhite people tend to view black men as more threatening than white men.[4]

The best way to get rid of your implicit bias is to *realize you have one* and then to seek reduce it. Meet more people and ask learning questions in a posture of humility to find out more about the cultures of others. If you don't have any black friends, make it a goal to meet one black person, then five, then ten, then a hundred. You won't be able to separate out false stereotypes from general trends until you have spent time in conversation with others. The process of getting rid of or reducing your implicit bias takes many years, so be patient and be committed.

EXTENDING HOSPITALITY ACROSS OLD LINES OF DIVISION

This list of things to do to build trust with people who are ethnically different than you may seem small and ordinary. But our lack of everyday interactions prevents us from getting to a place where we truly see each other, know each other, and can live in reconciliation with each other. Jesus modeled intentionality in interacting with non-Jews and brought his disciples into non-Jewish territory, making them uncomfortable and also forcing them to learn and ask new questions. Likewise, let us begin with the small steps needed to establish trust across ethnic barriers.

QUESTIONS FOR INDIVIDUAL REFLECTION AND SMALL GROUP DISCUSSION

1. What's your ethnic background? What foods or artifacts remind you of home or family?

2. Ask question number one of a couple friends who share your ethnic background and also those who are different from you. What did you learn or hear that you never knew before?

3. What message did you grow up hearing about different people groups? What family, community, educational, or media voices influenced such messages?

4. Who was seen as friendly?

5. Who was seen as untrustworthy or dangerous?

6. Who did you hear or receive very little messages about?

7. What is challenging about this chapter? What could you implement right away?

8. Who is someone that was a helpful teacher to you as you learned about other cultures? Why was it helpful?

RECOMMENDED READING

Cultural Intelligence: Improving Your CQ to Engage Our Multicultural World by David A. Livermore

Disunity in Christ: Uncovering the Hidden Forces That Keep Us Apart by Christena Cleveland

7

CROSSCULTURAL
SKILLS IN COMMUNITY

In *Cultural Intelligence*, David Livermore writes, "I'm confident most ministry leaders *want* to love the Other. But gaining the *ability* to love the Other and leading others in our ministries to do the same is the journey we're interested in."[1]

During a Bible study, I watched a white man earnestly try to engage by responding to the questions, sharing his thoughts, and having a mild debate about the topic. I could tell that he thought he was offering the best of himself. But I could also see that the Asian American woman in the group, who was quiet, wasn't very happy that the white man was always the first to speak and seemed to cut off others. I was sure she was thinking, *How dare he challenge the Bible study leader publicly! That is rude and unacceptable.* Meanwhile, I could see that the black woman in the group was not sure what to think of the Asian woman's disengagement from the discussion. *Was the woman checking out? How were they supposed to grow as a community if the woman seemed so closed off? And would this white man respond with some nonsense about colorblindness if I share my perspective as a black woman on the passage?*

The person leading the Bible study was hoping that the group would willingly share and grow deeper in community. What he didn't realize was that his leading method invited only those from expressive, low-hierarchy backgrounds. Inadvertently, he was reinforcing only one way of communicating. And he wasn't trying to figure out how the group might overcome its fears or anxieties.

Once we have the skills to build trust with non-Christians, we can invite people to the table of multiethnic fellowship in Jesus' name. But then we need to know *how* to be together at the table. We need to know how to communicate across cultures on a basic level. For many white Americans who grew up with mostly white friends, the learning curve is steep, as it is for Asian Americans who grew up in mostly Asian American circles or black Americans who grew up in mostly black circles. Crosscultural skills are needed in order to make a diverse, multiethnic community work.

I've often seen well-intentioned Christians and non-Christians alike assume that talking about diversity or ethnicity will help people live in multiethnic community. But the truth is, *people don't naturally know how to be friends across cultures*. Few of us are taught by our families how to have real friendships in diverse, multiethnic networks. Even our schools teach polite tolerance that never goes deep. The floundering Christian that makes a mess at the multiethnic table is not going to be a strong witness to a non-Christian, and he definitely will be an inhospitable guest.

THE CHALLENGE OF GROUP CULTURAL DIFFERENCES

Americans (no matter our ethnic variant) represent some of the most individualistic cultures in the world.[2] Individualism, the right to individual freedom and choices, makes many of us want to be seen at face value—as individuals not bound to a historical past or tethered to social hierarchy ("just call me Jane instead of Dr. Lee"). However, as you and your community experience the limitations of an individualistic framework, it will be harder to deny that you can represent a people and a history.

Let's say an ethnically diverse group of people including Asian, black, Latino, Middle Eastern, Native, and white Americans sit together to dine. Each individual could potentially represent an ethnic group that might have hurt another group represented at the table. You can't ask to be viewed for who you are as an individual because more than likely the people sitting across from you didn't receive the same treatment as an individual and instead were treated differently just because of the color of their skin. Everyone at the table communicates differently and has various values that might make conversation more difficult. In fact, some natural tendencies might only reinforce ethnic and racial scars.

Our ethnicities have cultural norms and values. Like an iceberg, there are cultural things you can see on the surface, such as food, dance, holiday traditions, customs, and language linked to a country or province of origin (though many would argue that language is the carrier of culture). On a deeper level (the nine-tenths of the iceberg below the surface of the water), culture encompasses so much more, such as notions of hospitality, fairness, relationships with authority and elders, physical touch, and communication (see figure 3). Culture can and does shift over time, and globalization and social media continue to affect it.

Regional cultures affect our expressions of our ethnic heritage cultures. For example, Texans have a distinctive flair, as do Southerners. Latinos from New York are different from those in Los Angeles. Midwestern and New England white people are different from each other. These cultures highlight and express different values, and we express our individual personalities in these cultures. How can we communicate across such values? More importantly, how do we invite a multiethnic group of people to the table where Jesus is the host?

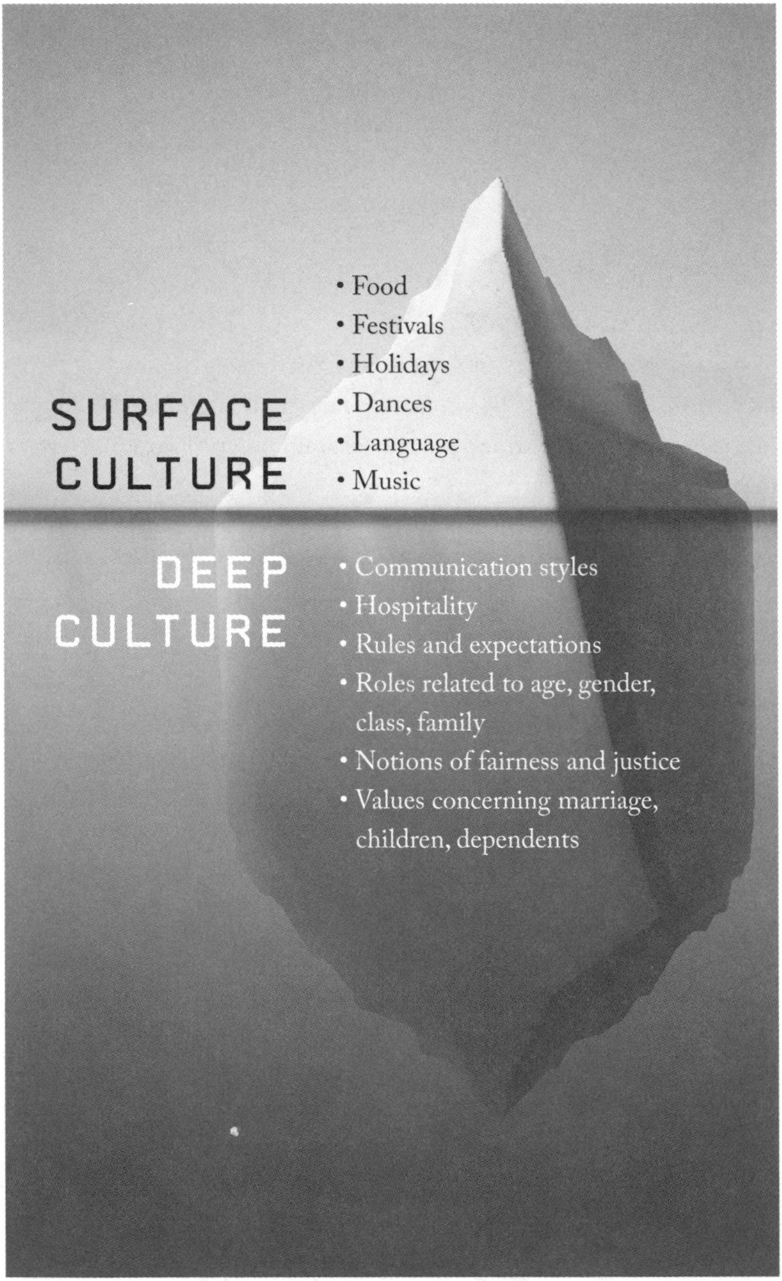

Figure 3. Surface culture versus deep culture

COMMUNICATING ACROSS DIFFERENT CULTURES

We must recognize that we communicate differently according to our ethnic cultures and backgrounds. Isaiah, a black man, was a leader in starting a witnessing community at a college. Isaiah is larger than life in size and personality—friendly to everyone, the center of attention. He was excited when he met a young Vietnamese American student named Luke who seemed to share Isaiah's excitement in reaching out to new people. Luke did every task Isaiah asked him to do. *He's so committed! This is great,* thought Isaiah. Then one day, Luke stopped showing up. Isaiah was confused and began to analyze what had happened. He realized that Luke wasn't saying yes because he believed in the vision of the group—Luke was saying yes because he was too polite to say no. Luke's actions honored his elder Isaiah, but Luke finally burned out because he kept avoiding the conflict of telling Isaiah otherwise. Isaiah, a direct person who expected to be treated more like a peer by someone like Luke (who was only three or four years younger than him), didn't understand the indirect ways Luke was trying to communicate with him. Luke respected Isaiah but wasn't committed to the vision for the group. There were value differences at play in this exchange. As you reach out to new communities, you'll encounter a diversity of values that differ from your own, including communication styles, power distance, and approaches to conflict.

Direct versus indirect communication styles. Isaiah took Luke's words at face value because he is familiar with direct, explicit communication, where what you say matters. In indirect communication, however, the *way* you say something matters just as much. My friend Dustin, a Taiwanese American, is notorious for answering "maybe" to something when he actually means "no." For many people from shame-based cultures (Asian, Latino, African, Native, Middle Eastern), saying no directly to someone's face is considered dishonoring to both parties.

High-power distance versus low-power distance. Power distance refers to your awareness of difference in age, social status, and position.

and how it affects your interactions with others. People with high-power distance will defer and give more authority to someone older or with more social status. People with low-power distance will think that peer friendship and casual interaction are possible with someone significantly older or younger than they are. Isaiah thought Luke was responding to his fun, energetic vision casting for the ministry, but in reality, Luke was dutifully trying to do what his "elder" asked him to do. In American culture, we talk about people becoming adults when they're eighteen. In Asian culture and many immigrant cultures, you are your parents' child until the day you die. Saying no to an elder has consequences and can lead to uncomfortable conflict and broken relationships.

Isaiah's story highlights a few of many possible value differences. Some of us are more motivated by individualism (individual goals and rights) while others are moved by collectivism (group goals and personal relationships). Still others of us think a democratic vote is a perfectly reasonable way of making a decision, while others of us don't feel comfortable unless consensus is reached by the whole group. Watch an Asian American church group try to decide where to eat for dinner. Everyone's desires and dislikes are considered, and the decision making process can take up to an hour. Obviously, collectivism and individualism as values overlap with either a consensus or democratic vote.

Books such as *Crossing Cultures with Jesus* or *Cross-Cultural Connections* emphasize the building of cultural intelligence and crosscultural skills. Don't just learn about differences between American and overseas culture. Also search out materials that help you learn about cultural differences within the United States.

Conflict acceptance versus conflict avoidance. Some of us come from cultures that are okay with having conflict, while others avoid it like the plague. Compare an Italian American with a Dutch American, or a Korean American with a Japanese American. The former (Italian and Korean) will tend to be more comfortable expressing conflict and difference of opinion and might even display changes in their tone of voice and emotion. The latter (Dutch and Japanese) might be put off by that communication style or view the conflict as a breaking of trust. Black American friends have often told me, "You know we trust you when we're willing to get real with you," which means they can be honest about their hurts and emotions without worrying about whether they sound like the stereotype of an angry black woman or man. But for a number of white and Asian people who are unaccustomed to big displays of emotions or direct confrontation, such conflicts can break trust.

Missional teams and communities that are diverse will need to shift in how they communicate with each other, how decisions are made, and in the expression of different values. Offering hospitality to each other allows us to be better at offering the hospitality of Christ to new communities.

BUT WHAT ABOUT BEING TRULY WHO I AM?

Being authentic to your ethnic self means not acting as if your cultural values are the norm. Assuming that your way is the way everyone should be, or assuming that you don't have to adjust when communicating with others, is a kind of cultural idolatry or self-worship. The people who learn to navigate crosscultural settings aren't being inauthentic: they're being good stewards of their ethnic identities to a diverse group of people.

You see this in Paul, the apostle to the Gentiles. He is vehemently opposed to circumcision as a means of proving one's salvation. When he returns to Jerusalem, he is advised to join with four men in a vow of purification rites and shaving heads (Acts 21:24). This way, the rest of the Jews will know that Paul isn't trying to destroy Judaism but is instead preaching about a Messiah who fulfills it. Paul complies. While Paul refuses to circumcise Titus, a Greek, to prove his salvation in Galatians 2, Paul is willing to have Timothy, a biracial Jewish and Greek man, circumcised. Is he being inauthentic by respecting the cultural norms and customs, or is he conveying respect and honor to the people that have yet to know Jesus?

When Paul goes to Philippi in Acts 16, he has to change his behavior. He can't find a synagogue, though his standard practice is to preach the gospel first to the Jews in a synagogue. So he goes to the river where Jews are gathered and finds Lydia, a wealthy vendor, at a women's prayer group. After she is baptized, Lydia insists, "If you consider me a believer in the Lord ... come and stay at my house" (Acts 16:15). Paul, who tries so hard to avoid being a burden, complies and goes with her, changing his usual behavior in order to be a good witness. That doesn't mean that he is being inauthentic.

As Jesus invites us to reach out to diverse people, we have to learn how to interact in ways that build trust, communicate honor, and extend hospitality. Instead of going to the synagogue, we might have to go to the river. This does not mean that we become less of ourselves. It means that we become more fully the people of God who invite others to the table.

LOOK FOR CULTURAL INTERPRETERS AND MENTORS

Find mentors and peers that will help you in this journey. Seek some peers and mentors who don't look like you and some who do look like you. Crosscultural interactions can shake up a number of things in us: our need for control, our desire to seem put together, perfectionism, and our fear of failure. It's disorienting if you're familiar with a low-power distance, verbally expressive white or black context and then you step into a room full of high-power distance Asian Americans where you might miss indirect hints or nonverbal cues. You can feel like a fish out of water. Instead of persisting in your blunders, ask for feedback from cultural interpreters, people who are willing to help you understand cultural differences between you and your setting.

If you regularly learn from someone who looks like you, seek out a mentor of a different ethnic background who will help you learn how to navigate their context. Learn from their stories, ask exploratory questions, and invite them to speak into your life. Seek out peer friendships where you can learn from people who are ethnically different from you. To be someone's token black or Latino friend is about appearances, not about the realness of crosscultural multiethnic community. It's not real friendship. Instead, genuinely invite people to speak into your life from their perspective.

Along with that, seek out mentors and peers of people from your ethnic background who have experience navigating deep crosscultural friendships and multiethnic community. Just as we learn much from people who are different than us, we learn a lot from people who share our backgrounds and are able to articulate how they were shaped, transformed, and challenged by their experiences and friendships in multiethnic community. These are few and far between, but you can pray that God brings those people into your life.

My husband, Shin, is Korean American. He spent time learning about the experiences of the black community in New Haven, Connecticut—a state with one of the widest disparities in incarceration rates between black and white residents.[3] As Shin was learning about black culture and systemic injustice and asking questions, he shared his fears of "urban people" with his black friends. They had journeyed with him in his learning process and looked at him with love and grace when they said, "Shin, you're not afraid of urban people. You're afraid of black people." Wow, talk about an honest comment! But this honest response prompted Shin to share about painful encounters he had as a child with black children on the playground. He realized he had internalized the racism done to him and was projecting that racism onto others. For example, one of Shin's knee-jerk reactions was to reach for his wallet every time he saw a black person get into an elevator with him. Shin's friend Alysia would gently squeeze his arm when this happened so that he was made aware of his prejudiced reactions. Over time, Shin was able to repent and intentionally work on his behavior and attitude about black people. Now, when Shin sees black folks, he has the opposite reaction, greeting them with warmth and enthusiasm. His black friends helped him overcome his prejudices.

You can identify a good mentor by watching them share how Jesus transformed their ethnic journeys. They know and embrace who they are ethnically; they can articulate the good in their culture, talk about their brokenness that Jesus is healing, and steward who they are for the kingdom.

I have learned much from my mentor Virginia, a pastor and seminary professor at Gordon-Conwell Theological Seminary. Virginia highly identifies with her black and Bajan (Barbados) identity. She'll break out into a Boston accent or start dancing to the soulful funk the band is playing as she leads us in worship. One wink from her can make you smile, and one stern look can make the most obstinate man fall silent. Some affectionately call her "the velvet hammer." Virginia navigates majority black, majority white, and multiethnic spaces by being herself. She also invites people into black sayings and humor instead of trying to deny her blackness in order to fit in. As she mentors women and men of other ethnicities, she shares with me what she is learning about cultural and ethnic differences and how it's reflected in her leadership. Her intentional leadership helps me understand how to navigate a multiethnic world.

Another mentor is James, who is Korean American like me. James is so friendly and winsome he could probably be friends with anyone. I've seen him navigate crosscultural spaces without denying his ethnic self and share stories about his ethnic heritage in rooms that are mostly non-Korean. James tells his real stories. He knows his ethnicity is valuable and shares from his life in ways that connect with people even if they are not Korean. Once he said, "Too often, Asian Americans define ourselves by our weaknesses and faults. It's time we started to define ourselves by our strengths and beauty." As he reflects on what he is learning and how he is navigating crosscultural spaces, I learn from his experiences. James helped me see how I could be a Korean American, Christian, female leader.

As we draw from the rich experiences of mentors and friends and intentionally learn the skills needed to become ethnically aware, we become more hospitable members of the multiethnic family of God. Ethnicity-aware living allows us to become more hospitable to those close and far from God as we enter into different settings and learn more about people. Ethnicity-aware living helps build trust so that a non-Christian of a different ethnic background can trust us both as a Christian and as someone who is ethnically different.

SKILLS FOR COMMUNICATING IN GROUPS

As our social, work, and church circles become increasingly more diverse, here are some starter tips for communicating in diverse groups.

Look up, speak second. I went on a summer missions trip with a group of white and Asian American women and men. When our group was asked a question during orientation, I noticed that the white participants would look up and immediately start sharing. The Asian American participants would first look around to see if they were going to cut anyone off as they answered. This led to the persistent cutting off of the Asian American members by the white members. Both were trying to participate the way they knew best: the former by offering their ideas and opinions and the latter by making space for others to share. When I pointed this out, the group was surprised! So we implemented a general principle of "look up, speak second," which allowed more people to join the discussions, including our Ugandan team members that would join us later in Kampala.

Use numbers to gauge the strength of opinions. Saying something such as, "Why don't we do this?" can sound either like a suggestion or a strong conviction, based on the hearer. When supervising Asian American men and women, I have to be careful that I'm clear in my communication.

Because the Asian American culture is a high-power distance culture, they are likely to do what I tell them (or figure out a way to go around me). So if I'm stating an idea, I usually say, "I think we should do this for our community event. I'm a three out of ten." If I'm stating a strong opinion, I say instead, "I think we should do this for our community event. I'm a nine out of ten." Using a statement plus a number scale invites the more indirect or hesitant members of your group to share their insights and lets you hear ideas from a broader range of people.

Gathering input: "fist to five." In conversation, the loudest and most opinionated voice can be overruling. However, the repeat pattern of the most dominant personality determining group decisions can feel oppressive, limiting, and inhospitable. If you're making a group decision about something, whether it's as small as where to go eat or as big as making ministry structural changes, you need to get input beyond the loudest voice. Avoid the assumption that silence means agreement or consensus. I have been in many settings where ethnic minorities or women do not speak up much, and it's often construed as agreement versus something else (silent disagreement, fear of presenting a dissenting opinion, or an internal, silencing voice of self-critique). Try this instead: let's say your group is making a decision, and you want to gauge the actual ownership of the decision from everyone. Ask, "On a scale of zero to five, how comfortable do you feel with our decision? Please show via your fingers (a fist meaning zero, or very uncomfortable; five fingers meaning five, or very comfortable)." Ask them to show their votes all at the same time ("Vote on the count of three") so they don't feel pressured by others' opinions on display.

If the group shows mostly fours and fives, the group is on the same page. If the group shows mostly fours and fives but there are one or two outliers that show lower numbers, pause and (respectfully) ask them why they feel that way. When the dissenting voices are of the ethnic minority in the group, this method helps pinpoint where cross-cultural differences might be getting in the way of making a decision.

Doing "fist to five" allows you to identify opinions that might otherwise be silent. Seeing an individual or a whole group show twos and threes might hurt, but then you get to ask the next question: "What would it take to make it a five?" or "What it would it take from each of us to make it a five?" Especially in teams that are committed to a common objective, this allows people to not just focus on the gap but also to contribute ideas and cultural influences.

Vary group discussion. If you're used to leading in a way that invites the most expressive and uninhibited people to speak up, try to vary your leadership technique. Break people off into small groups (pairs or triads) and have them share with each other. Ask them to appoint a spokesperson to share on behalf of their group.

In one meeting, my friend Larry tried to encourage more sharing from men and women of color by asking the white men and women in the room to wait until others had spoken. I predicted what happened next: "Did most of the black men and women speak up but not many Asian Americans?" I asked. "Yes! How did you know?" he responded. Larry was using freeform discussion in the large group. Instead, he should have broken people into triads and asked them to appoint spokespersons. This allows for the ethnic diversity of the spokespersons to broaden and for more people to engage in dialogue. When a non-Christian in a group is the spokesperson, it affirms their seeking and can help deepen their understanding of Scripture.

Another way to encourage discussion is to go around in a circle or start with the youngest or the eldest in the room (depending on which age demographic may end up being the least heard). And every ethnic background has reflective thinkers that need time to process their thoughts internally before sharing them. I remember leading a Bible study with a non-Christian who asked after a couple meetings, "Could you email us the questions beforehand? It helps me to have more time to think."

SKILLS FOR BUILDING TRUST IN
A MULTIETHNIC COMMUNITY

Multiethnic community involves extending hospitality across cultural differences. It also involves being aware of racial history and context while honoring the other. Here are some things that you can do to help build trust in a multiracial, multiethnic community.

Use a prophetic instead of an accusatory voice. Everyone is a learner, and that means that everyone is going to make mistakes as they interact in multiethnic community. If you define someone by only their mistakes, you are telling them that they themselves are that mistake.

We must choose to be prophetic instead of accusatory. An accusatory voice says, "Look at this thing you did wrong! You *are wrong!*" It uses shame, fear, and anxiety to motivate change. It promotes self-protection and is usually unsuccessful in the long run. A prophetic voice says, "This is not who God is calling you to be. You could be so much more than this broken behavior. Come and follow Jesus into that hope."

As we teach each other to be in multiethnic community, and particularly as white Americans are taught to be in multiethnic community, it's important to affirm a positive identity and maintain a vision of what could be, instead of naming the person by their unintentional (or sometimes intentional) mistake only. Saying, "You're a racist because you said this racist comment," will bring up denial or extreme apology. It doesn't help the person change for better. Instead, saying, "I know you care about loving your community, and that you're more than that comment; it hurts in this way: _____. How can it be different next time?" points to change and the person that *could be*.

My husband experienced this as a child in rural New Jersey, when an elderly white woman in his neighborhood called him *Oriental*. He gently corrected her by saying, "I'm sorry to interrupt, but I wanted to let you know that *Oriental* is not the correct way to refer to my people.

You should call us *Asian*. *Oriental* refers to furniture, and it's an offensive label because it was originally a term meant to describe Asians as unwanted 'others' from a foreign place. Could you use *Asian* in the future?"

The woman was genuinely surprised because no one had ever corrected her, and *Oriental* had been an accepted term in her white community for some sixty years. "Thank you for telling me! I would never have known," was her response. She always made it a point to use the word *Asian* instead of *Oriental* in future conversations with him.

What would happen if every time you heard a person (white or nonwhite) make a mistake or say something offensive, you didn't talk about what they did wrong and instead focused on what could be? Instead of failures, you would see students, people who could learn with you. Cultural learning is not a trophy to be waved around like a flag or bragging rights. It's something that's meant to be shared. And this is not just a specific task for white folks. We all need to learn about what it means to be in a multiethnic community.

If you're starting this journey from zero, embrace that reality instead of being ashamed of it. Debrief your experiences with a safe person, someone who is willing to teach you and give feedback about your interactions with them and others in a multiethnic community. This kind of invitation builds far more trust than trying to be perfect on your own (which actually isn't possible). Perfection is never something the Lord demanded of us. Faithfulness and perseverance are the only requirements. Ask Jesus for the courage to learn, and find some trustworthy people to help you grow.

Talk about an ethnically inclusive God and his story. As we share the good news and reflect upon the story of God, it's important to use a variety of images to represent God. Much imagery of Jesus casts him as a blond, blue-eyed white man carrying a lamb. However, Jesus was Middle Eastern and probably looked Palestinian! If we continue the practice of showing Jesus as white, we fall into the idolatry of prizing whiteness above others. God created us in ethnic diversity—no one culture captures his goodness or character perfectly. Try to vary the images you use so that you don't communicate that God is a god of white people only or that you need to be white in order to be included in the kingdom of God. Representing Jesus as white is not bad. Just make sure you don't emphasize a bias toward whiteness and instead include white as one of many options.

My mother has a book by a Korean artist that includes drawings of the gospel of Matthew. Every scene, from Bethlehem to Calvary, depicts Jesus as ethnically Korean because the artist wanted to make the gospel more accessible to his people. Likewise, in your stories and sermon illustrations, make sure the protagonist is not always one ethnicity. In particular, be careful about always depicting white people as the heroes while black and brown people are the villains. Use stories with heroes from a variety of ethnicities.

In your signage and visual media, include people of every ethnicity—and I don't just mean six white people and one black person, which is visual tokenism. Small things go a long way to communicate intentionality and hospitality to people of color. On the flip side, there are majority black and Asian churches that intentionally try to communicate welcome to white and nonwhite people that are the minority in their community by using photos and stories that include them in their communal life. Communicate who you desire to be.

If you're a ministry leader preparing a sermon or a study, seek to learn from and be influenced by teachings from more than one ethnic group (particularly if the group has previously heard from primarily white men). Reflect the diversity of the church in the United States and globally in your quotes and references to theologians and Christian examples.

Honor and be tender toward the formerly dishonored parts. When Paul wrote in 1 Corinthians 12:23, "The parts [of the body] that we think are less honorable we treat with special honor," he was well aware that he was speaking to a diverse Corinthian church, full of Jews and Gentiles, slaves and free. In the Roman Empire, the most dishonored population would likely have been the poor, unskilled slaves. In the United States, we have a sad history of people of color being dishonored through systemic racism and prejudice, and we need to recognize that.

Many white Americans that come from low-power distance families don't like being called "sir" or "ma'am" because they don't want to be reminded of their advancing age. But for many people of color and immigrant cultures that place value in age-based social hierarchy, "sir" or "ma'am" honors the older people's status as elders. Given that much of American history has dishonored black men and women, I say "sir" and "ma'am" to convey respect toward black elders that I meet. Though I am Asian American (not white), I represent people who have either had negative interactions with black Americans, avoided them, or stereotyped them according to negative media projections.

Honoring is different from reinforcing tropes or stereotypes. Honoring says, "You are of great value to God and therefore to me." In big and small gestures, honoring the other affirms them as being made in the image of God. So whether it's greeting with respect an elder whose ethnicity is different from your own or extending hospitality toward an ethnic other, do so knowing that you are extending shalom across a history of racial scars and division.

Meet guests in their sadness about ethnic pain or injustice. Sometimes the guests at your table will bring stories of sadness or pain, particularly as it relates to their ethnic people. And if your hospitality is truly about hosting them well and not just about having a nice diverse experience, you will host them in their sadness. Daisy is a Harvard Divinity School student, a Latina from California. She was born in Mexico but grew up in the United States undocumented. We invited her and her boyfriend, Frank, to dinner after church, along with a group of white people they didn't know. When Daisy was asked how she was doing, she answered that she was sad. She recently took a trip to Arizona to understand the policies and procedures regarding the capture of undocumented immigrants, most of whom were Latin American. She talked about how many people cross the desert and die of dehydration, how Native American reservation communities report undocumented immigrants because they don't want police raids in their community (though others leave water jugs to help such travelers), and about how the immigrants get sent to prison and then undergo expedited removal back to the land from which they were trying to escape.

My husband and the white friends at dinner didn't know what to say other than, "We know so little about this. Thank you for sharing with us." We felt the heaviness of Daisy's sorrow. And for Daisy, it was a gift to share with a group of Asian and white strangers-turned-friends who were willing to listen. It made us want to learn more and understand the complexity of issues surrounding immigration. It built trust between Daisy, Frank, and my white friends because we didn't run away or change the subject. We were communicating that they were welcome at the table just as they were, in their beauty and scars.

Shortly after the shooting death of black teenager Michael Brown by a white police officer in Ferguson, Missouri, that led to community unrest, I reached out to John, a black man who is a member of our mostly Asian and white church. "How are you doing with everything happening with Ferguson? How can our church be praying for you?" John's eyes welled up with tears as he said, "It just means so much that you would ask." During a prayer vigil, my husband and I wept alongside of John as he shared about the painful conversations he would need to have with his soon-to-be teenage son and the fears he had for his son's safety. John and I are in different life stages, different ethnic groups, and entirely different realms of work. But because my husband and I were willing to listen, sit with, and pray with John, it cemented a depth of trust between us.

We can't avoid the sadness and pain that our brothers and sisters of different backgrounds face navigating a racially and ethnically broken world. My husband and I sit with white friends who weep and wrestle with difficult experiences, times when they messed up or were misunderstood as white women and men. We make space for Latino friends to share their struggles. We give space to friends who need to grieve on their own or with their people before they are ready to talk. Hospitality is about creating a home where you can be safe, cared for, and loved by your spiritual family without having to pretend like everything is okay.

QUESTIONS FOR INDIVIDUAL REFLECTION AND SMALL GROUP DISCUSSION

1. Name a time where you felt like a fish out of water in a cultural context that was different than your own. What was that like for you? What happened? What would you do differently next time?

2. What are some crosscultural communication skills and habits that you could try out in the future? What questions do you have?

3. Who are the Christian authors and theologians who influence you the most? What do you notice about their ethnic backgrounds?

4. Who are some mentors and cultural interpreters that can help you navigate multiethnic community?

RECOMMENDING READING

Cross-Cultural Connections: Stepping Out and Fitting In Around the World by Duane Elmer

Crossing Cultures with Jesus: Sharing Good News with Sensitivity and Grace by Katie J. Rawson

Crossing Cultures in Scripture: Biblical Principles for Mission Practice by Marvin J. Newell

8

RESPONDING TO CROSSCULTURAL CONFLICT IN COMMUNITY

Kelly was getting her student leaders ready to do a major outreach on campus. They had large, colorful posters and spiritual surveys ready. Their fellowship had spent many months talking about ethnicity, race, the Black Lives Matter movement, and racial injustice. They were going to ask people on campus what they thought about race relations on the campus and in the country. Kelly was hopeful that the room of around one hundred Asian, white, Latino, and black American students would be a powerful multiethnic witness to the campus. Kelly asked the leaders how they felt about starting such conversations, and many shared honestly about their fears and excitement. A young, white, first-year student named Mandy shared, "I'm scared and not sure if I know how to do this well."

Suddenly, seemingly out of nowhere, one of the black leaders declared, "How am I supposed to trust this room to have the right conversations with black students on campus?" Pointing at Mandy, the black leader exclaimed, "She doesn't even know what she's talking about!"

Time seemed to stop for Kelly, who had been praying for her community to be able to reach out to a campus that was hurting because of racial conflict. She thought they were ready, but an unexpected crosscultural conflict had erupted. What to do?

This conflict would plunge Kelly and her leaders into deeper listening and knowing of each other. It exposed the reality that several
new leaders were unfamiliar with the months of conversation and
trust that had been built previously. They needed to pause and figure
out what was happening. It forced them to have conversations that
they hadn't known they needed to have, addressing fears and division.
In the end, the dialogue, apologies, and reconciliation that resulted
made them even stronger. Conflict didn't negate the realness of their
multiethnic community. They're not perfect, and their community
continues to be a work in progress. But these types of conversations
help them address new realities, barriers, and opportunities that come
with being a growing missional, multiethnic community.

Many organizations, churches, and universities use a stereotypically
predictable image for their brochures and websites to convey the great
diversity of their community: a photo of smiling white, black, Asian,
and Latino Americans enjoying a conversation or laughing together.
Organizations and universities use these types of photos to convey
that they are a diverse environment, keeping with the times. But this
is often little more than *multicolored attendance.*

A bunch of people from diverse backgrounds sitting together for
an activity (be it a class, worship service, or conference) is not auto-
matically a multiethnic community. Many of our colleges, organizations, and even churches have a multicultural space celebrating cultural diversity, but very few have spaces that are able to endure together
racial and crosscultural conflict, both internal and external to the
community. Many universities have an office for multicultural affairs
but not one that addresses racial relationships. The rainbow of cultural
colors is often little more than a false or shallow understanding of
multiethnic community.

A multiethnic community is defined by relationships that are
marked by trust and commitment able to persevere through conflict.
On the other hand, multicolored attendance is a shallow celebration

of the visual semblance of togetherness. When tensions arise, holding hands and singing "Kumbaya" is not enough to hold together a hollow, multicolored attendance community.

ACTS 6: DIVISION ALONG HISTORIC CULTURAL TENSIONS

There are few things more painful to a Christian community than a church spilt, and in Acts 6, we see the potential beginnings of one. We read, "In those days when the number of disciples was increasing, the Hellenistic Jews among them complained against the Hebraic Jews because their widows were being overlooked in the daily distribution of food" (Acts 6:1).

In our American Western context of abundance, this can be misread as a small but embarrassing logistical oversight that could be fixed by providing more food at the next potluck. But we need to understand the cultural context to know what's at stake.

Six centuries before Jesus was born, Israel was conquered by the Assyrians and Babylonians, who were then conquered by the Persians, who were conquered by the Greeks, after which the Romans took over. When the Greeks ruled, Israel's culture and spiritual lineage were attacked. Antiochus, eager to find financial means of offering tribute to the powers that be, sold the high priesthood (a title that Jews reserved only for descendants of Aaron). A man named Jason bought the priesthood for 27,000 pounds of silver and forced a Hellenistic lifestyle onto the Jews by implementing Greek gymnasiums, Greek educational systems, and the worship of Greek gods (see 2 Maccabees 4:7-14). Antiochus slaughtered a pig at the altar in the temple, pocketed temple money, and put many to death, including punishing mothers who had circumcised their babies by killing the babies and hanging the corpses around their mothers' necks (see 1 Maccabees 1:47, 60-61). The Jews found relief in the Maccabean family, who helped to end Greek rule. But eventually, Israel was humbled by the return of Roman rule, which amplified much of the Greeks' cultural and educational practices and publicly crucified thousands (robbers and freedom-fighters alike). Jesus' crucifixion was a commonplace execution, one of many for failed leaders of revolts. The early church grew out of Jewish roots in a world that had been Hellenized for centuries.

Hellenistic Jews had adopted Greek language, customs, and culture. Hebraic Jews retained Hebrew customs, language, and culture in the face of hundreds of years of persecution, torture, and death. This tension is at work in Acts 6. When both the Hellenistic Jews and the Hebraic Jews became Christ followers, they brought this history of conflict with them.

In this culture, widows needed alms and protection from charitable individuals to survive. So in Acts 6:1, the complaint is not just about needing food for a one-time meal. It's about people wrestling with daily poverty.

Acts 6 represents a potential church split due to crosscultural tension and distrust, a ministry leader's worst nightmare. What would you do if you were in this situation? If you represented the Hebraic Jews that were being well served, how would you expect the offended Hellenistic Jews to respond? Updating it to today, how would you respond if black members of your mostly white church raised concerns that most of the Bible studies and church sermons seemed catered toward white people?

ACTS 6: A RESPONSE OF FAITH

Here's the next part of the story:

> So the Twelve gathered all the disciples together and said, "It would not be right for us to neglect the ministry of the word of God in order to wait on tables. Brothers and sisters, choose seven men from among you who are known to be full of the Spirit and wisdom. We will turn this responsibility over to them

and will give our attention to prayer and the ministry of
the word."

This proposal pleased the whole group. They chose Stephen,
a man full of faith and of the Holy Spirit; also Philip, Procorus,
Nicanor, Timon, Parmenas, and Nicolas from Antioch, a convert
to Judaism. They presented these men to the apostles, who
prayed and laid their hands on them. (Acts 6:2-6)

Instead of becoming defensive, avoidant, or combative, the Twelve
disciples gather the leaders of the church together and are willing to
hear the concerns and pain of their community. They respond by identifying new leaders who are marked by obedience to the Holy Spirit
and pray over them to confirm that these are the right people to lead.

The specific men chosen as leaders is significant, as they were all
Hellenistic Jews. These men were to be in charge of feeding not just
the Hellenistic widows but all of the widows. In the secular world, and
even in the church world, this may be considered ludicrous. Wouldn't
the Hellenist men just even the score by giving their community more
food than the Hebraic Jews? Instead, the leaders trust the seven men,
who set about the tremendous task given to them. Will the Hebraic
Jewish widows and community trust them? Is this enough to repair
the damage that has been done?

A fear that comes up for many ministry leaders is that becoming
more diverse will cause people to leave. I was a part of a Korean
Christian Fellowship that was debating about becoming more pan-
Asian in name to reflect the Chinese and Taiwanese non-Christian
friends we were trying to reach. Many people were concerned about
the Korean people feeling uncomfortable, and indeed, some people
did leave. But our Christian communities should not be about feeling
comfortable. As we learned how to be more inclusive, the community
grew. In multiethnic missional community, everyone ends up being a
little uncomfortable for the sake of making room for the other.

If you lead your ministry out of a place of fear of what people think, remember that ultimately you answer only to the Lord. And if you have concerns about how people will get along, remember that you can and should teach them how. You can't just throw them into a room together and hope for the best (like throwing a couple of firecrackers into a room with a lit match and crossing your fingers). We don't know for sure, but given these dynamics, my guess is that the leaders in Acts 6 gently reminded the group that Jesus welcomed all, Samaritans and Gentiles alike, and therefore they needed to do the same. So what happened next?

ACTS 6: THE FRUIT OF RECONCILIATION IN WITNESS

After the decision is made to appoint new leaders, the church continues to grow: "So the word of God spread. The number of disciples in Jerusalem increased rapidly, and a large number of priests became obedient to the faith" (Acts 6:7).

We could suppose that the problem with the widows was just a logistical hump for the superstar apostles to get over so that they could focus on their mission-advancing preaching, but notice the last part of the verse: "A large number of priests became obedient to the faith."

Priests were a part of the temple system and understood Hebrew customs and traditions. As the leaders of the Hebraic Jews, they knew the kind of community that Yahweh had taught the Israelites to be: united as one, feeding widows, caring for orphans, and quick to resolve differences. Could they have seen the solution with the widows as an example of united witness, trust, correction, and partnership in feeding the poor, and thought, *These Christians are able to do what living by Torah alone could not*? Here, they saw a community of God persevere through cultural tension and conflict that separated so many Jews. The response of the Acts church strengthened their witness to the Jewish community.

By caring for Hellenistic Jews, the Acts church saw Hebraic Jewish leaders become Christians. Crosscultural conflict and chaos became an opportunity to invite in the Holy Spirit and live united. Later in Acts 7 and 8, the seven new leaders are not just responsible for the widows but also become part of the rapidly expanding ministry of the church.

In Acts 6, God turns a chaos moment into a *kairos* moment. The believers are marked by a deep trust of each other and of God, which in turn yields a willingness to work through conflict, making room for new leaders. Multiethnic community drives the mission forward to all communities that could be blessed by the church.

What can we take away from Acts for our current context? Oftentimes, ministries and churches settle for multicolored attendance and avoid talking about crosscultural conflict and racial tension—or avoid attempting to diversify the ministry altogether. But it's a lie that you must sacrifice white Christians in order to reach more people of color. It's also a lie that you must sacrifice people of color in order to reach white Christians. Fear and anxiety should not limit our mission fields.

It takes discernment, prayerfulness, and a willingness to learn intentional hospitality for a multiethnic community to reach all people more effectively. So when crosscultural conflict occurs, we can apply the following four strategies.

ALWAYS PAY ATTENTION TO HISTORICAL CONTEXT

As much as you might want to be valued based on your merits alone by someone of a different ethnic background, you do represent the history of a macro-ethnic people group. Be aware of the history of interactions between your ethnicity and others and take care to honor those who have been dishonored by your people. Extend an intercessional apology where appropriate.

Clement, a Taiwanese American, was visiting his brother's majority white church. To his chagrin, the church used Chinese-like music (gongs, pentatonic scale jingles, high-pitched martial arts yelling) and ninja references based on stereotypes in a video and sermon. While everyone around him laughed, Clement felt like he wanted to be invisible. When Clement encouraged his brother to write the pastoral team about his concerns, they responded, "We asked an Asian person if they thought it was okay, and they said it was. So we don't think it was a problem."

Instead of listening, the pastoral team responded with defensiveness and denial. They lacked an understanding of how hurtful Asian stereotypes have been for Asian Americans. They asked only one person about it, not realizing that the person wasn't racially aware enough of the history of their people to be able to give proper feedback. The ministry leaders should have asked several Asian Americans who were more knowledgeable about the larger context. Instead, the church created an inhospitable space for Asian Americans.

If you are a white man mentoring a younger black man, you need to be aware of the historical interactions he and his family might have had with white men and women. You need to check your interactions with the young man and make sure that you're not behaving in a way that enforces falsehoods based on his ethnicity and cultural expression of the gospel.

If you want your community to be more welcoming to people who are in the minority, you need to equip your team to be hospitable. Extend kindness and intentionality that is countercultural to what the secular world offers. Pray and ask God for help, and ask him to provide people who are knowledgeable and can teach you.

When you hear that a community is reeling from a hate crime or when national crises regarding race fill your news feed, don't ignore it. Silence can look like complicity, where you're saying either it's okay or it doesn't matter. Make space to acknowledge the pain and pray for the victims and perpetrators involved. The reality is that we are not in a post-racial, colorblind society. A number of nationally publicized deaths of black men, women, and children have occurred in the past few years, and the ugliness of the 2016 election exposed some shocking racialized attitudes. We should acknowledge that we live in a context very similar to the Acts 6 church and be marked by their same sensitivity to the Holy Spirit.

BE QUICK TO LISTEN IN CULTURAL CONFLICT AND RACIAL TENSION

The apostles were *not* defensive or argumentative when the Hellenistic Jewish community raised their concerns about the widows. Instead, they made space for people to feel heard and convened a prayer and leadership meeting based on those concerns. When tension comes up on your team or ministry, make space to listen to the community and respond thoughtfully. Listen to the Holy Spirit in prayer; the Spirit will guide you about next steps, about where to apologize, where to change course, and what to say next. It's hard to hear Holy Spirit's voice if you're weighed down by fear, shame, or anxiety, so confess those feelings and ask the Lord for guidance. Read Acts 6:1-7 to remember that God is bigger than the conflict in your team and that he deeply cares about the local or national crises in your midst. Ask him to repair and restore trust that is broken, and invite your community into reconciliation and united witness.

When crosscultural conflict or a racial tension arise, it's an opportunity to ask the Lord, *What would you have me do?* Don't avoid or minimize the situation, but be willing to stand alongside the hurting and broken. Show humility in asking for feedback about how you could change to be more inclusive and effective in your interactions with more people. Be willing to prayerfully partner with those whose cultures and communication styles are vastly different from your own.

Different ministry leaders have asked me how to help those under their leadership respond to the pain experienced by the black community in the aftermath of the recent highly publicized deaths of several black people at the hands of police. In my experience, you can preach about systemic injustice and white privilege, but I don't think this is the most effective way of inviting people to *care*. If you teach people about theory and concepts, overloading them with facts, they stay only until they're tired or burned-out.

The most loving thing to do is show up and listen, without judgment. We can ask leaders to make space to care for the hurting. Our communities need to steward Christ's call to be a caring member of the body of Christ. Stewardship of leadership is a concept that is immediately applicable. As people hear others' stories, they start to see patterns of systemic injustice that affect communities of color. Because they've had real conversations with real people and friends, they stay for the long haul. What would you not do for your friend, whose heart you know so intimately that when it bleeds, yours aches too?

If you're the one bringing up the conflict, the following general principles are helpful. A general rule of thumb in conflict is to use "I" language instead of "you" language. Avoid globalizing and accusatory language such as "you *never*" or "you *always*." It's one thing to say, "You *never* acknowledge people of color!" while it's another thing to say, "I have noticed that we don't do the best job of acknowledging people of color in the room."

The Situation-Behavior-Impact (SBI) tool is also helpful to use in conflict.[1] It helps us ground our discussion of conflict in concrete situations and specific details instead of in generalizations and assumptions that can be hard to follow and understand, especially across cultural differences.

Situation: Describe the context/situation where the observed behavior occurred.

- "When our team met yesterday to plan our conference . . ."

- "When we were hanging out yesterday . . ."

Behavior: Describe the specific behavior that was hurtful, insensitive, or problematic.

- "I noticed that all but one of the speakers were white."

- "You made a passing joke imitating a bad Chinese accent."

Impact: Describe the impact it on you and/or others (as well as possible future impact).

- "I'm concerned that we're not being more intentional in diversifying our leadership for this important event. I don't think it feels hospitable to people of color who are considering attending."

- "If Mei Lin was in the room, I think she would have been hurt. I think it would have been offensive to her."

Finally, offer an alternative.

- "I know we want to see our organization grow and reach more people. Could we consider incorporating more diverse leadership?"

- "You're my friend. I know you don't want to hurt people. Can we avoid those kind of jokes in the future?"

Most importantly, pray. Prayer helps us hear from God in the midst of conflict. If both parties are praying, the chances of God speaking and bringing resolution are much higher.

BE QUICK TO APOLOGIZE AND SEEK RECONCILIATION

In Acts 6, the apostles immediately respond to their community by putting a plan into action. Their behavior shows that they recognized something was wrong. We can imagine that there was probably far more to their meeting than what's described in Acts 6:2. Maybe they reflected on what Jesus had done and told them to do: go out and make disciples of all nations. Perhaps they discussed and concluded that it was not Christ-like to show favoritism to the Hebraic Jewish widows. They may have apologized to those who had been hurt particularly by this oversight.

The secular world does not expect leaders to ever admit to being wrong. When they do, it is often revealed by force, and they are made to step down. There are some cases of serious sin that make it appropriate for a ministry leader to resign and seek counseling, healing, and restoration. But the leader that is quick to admit shortcomings and seek reconciliation even in the smaller things exhibits a responsiveness and humility that is actually quite attractive. This is different from an "I hate myself" kind of self-flagellating apology. The apology is about a concrete action that was taken or not taken.

I taught on Acts 6 at a training conference on missional multiethnicity. During the training and without my prompting, the two senior leaders, white men in their forties, asked if they could speak to the seventy people present. With tears in their eyes, they said, "As your leaders, we wanted to apologize. One, we're sorry that we didn't prioritize ethnic diversity as we've pursued planting and reaching new communities. And two, we're sorry for making our workplace a difficult and painful space for our colleagues of color." Their staff had been particularly affected by the recent injustices and protests in Ferguson, Missouri. I could not have asked for better timing or content more in line with the spirit of Acts 6. The leaders' apologies were specific and substantial, and they submitted themselves to their community. Their staff gathered around them, offered forgiveness, and prayed that the Lord would increase the leadership and wisdom of these two men. Many senior leaders of color were deeply moved by this public confession and individually prayed blessings over them. It delighted me to hear that, in the months after the training, this ministry was reaching more black students than they ever had before and had also started planting a strategic outreach to Native American students.

When we confess our failures and gaps, we give space for the Holy Spirit to come into those formerly secret parts to begin healing. We give space for repentance, forgiveness, grace, and deeper partnership. If you never ask for forgiveness for missteps in crosscultural friendships or in leading ministry, something is wrong. You either have not admitted that you make mistakes, or people don't trust you enough to be willing to confront you! We don't need to be perfect; we just need to be open to the deep touch of the Perfect One who is Christ, who heals us while shaping us into his image.

MAKE SPACE FOR STRONG PARTNERS OF DIVERSE BACKGROUNDS

Crosscultural conflict often exposes our biases and the people we might be unintentionally excluding. Inviting the perspectives and leadership of men and women who are ethnically different from you will help you better lead and respond to leadership challenges in a multiethnic witnessing community. They might not look or sound like you, but if they are marked by Christ-like leadership, prayerfulness, and the respect of their ethnic community, they are very strong potential partners. If your community is diverse but your leadership team is all white (or all Asian, black, or Latino American), you're missing some key perspectives about how to effectively minister to your whole congregation. Invite feedback from people who are underrepresented in your group. If you're trying to diversify your leadership team, your board, or your staff team, find someone who is respected and trusted by people of color (as well as white members). Give them responsibilities that matter, and walk with them as they try new things and help your community grow.

Acts 6 shows that in the kingdom of God, power is not a zero-sum game. The apostles make space for more leaders, and they trust those new leaders with an important task. Make room for more leaders in your context, be it a new position or in making sure that the next elected leaders represent a broader range of the people you are trying to reach with the gospel.

And stand by these leaders, advocate for them, and set them up for success. I've heard many sad stories about churches or organizations that invited a black, Latino, or Asian American member onto their mostly white staff, but underestimated how difficult it would be for that person as they navigated difficult interactions with other members and tried to fit into a dominantly white way of doing things. They found that the people who invited them just wanted to *look* diverse; they didn't want to change how things were run. If you invite someone onto a team that is ethnically different from the team, and particularly if that person is the ethnic minority, train your group on what to say and not to say (have them read chapters six and seven). Ask that person for feedback and check in on how they're doing. Take their ideas and feedback seriously. Continue to diversify your leadership team. In *Roadmap to Reconciliation*, Brenda Salter McNeil writes that many organizations and churches assume that initial diversification means success. But without structural intentionality, initial changes have little lasting impact.[2]

When the apostles chose the seven leaders in Acts 6, they gave them leadership position and influence over the entire group. Make sure that you're not inviting people to be just visual placeholders. Don't ask a black or Asian American speaker to be the token voice on race. This is a common complaint from many ministry leaders of color. Defy that stereotyping norm. Ask them to speak on things other than race or ethnicity, such as faithfulness, prayer, suffering, or other aspects of life with Christ. Their leadership, grounded in who they are and their ethnic background, is a gift for all.

THE DREAM

It's hard work to be a reconciling, ethnicity aware community! It involves growing a larger set of skills, being aware of what's at stake, and having the humility to admit wrongdoing. We all will make mistakes like the Acts 6 church did. If we can model and teach our Christian communities to pay attention to historical context, to be quick to listen, to apologize in places of wrong, to seek reconciliation, and to make space for diverse leadership, we stand a much better chance at becoming a persevering, multiethnic witnessing community.

In the beginning of this chapter, we read about Kelly, a white woman faced with the task of leading a diverse leadership community through public crosscultural conflict. However, Kelly was able to keep her cool because she had navigated such tension before. Several months earlier, the group had spent time talking about the issues of injustice affecting black men and women. Her Latino student-leaders, who were of the minority in her large leadership team, told her that they felt unseen and unheard in the conversation about race, particularly because the issues about immigration and racism toward Latinos was real and present in Southern California. Kelly invited them to share about how painful it was to hear the insensitive comments from the 2016 presidential campaigns about Latinos because it highlighted their daily reality of dealing with racism and prejudice. And they spoke of how they felt unseen in a group that talked so much about black people. The community listened to the Latino students and responded with humility and repentance rather than defensiveness. The group asked for forgiveness and asked Jesus for change as they prayed. The Latino leaders were amazed and emboldened in their witness as a result. Renewed with missional vision and conviction, they went out on the campus and shared about a Jesus who sees Latinos and calls them to freedom in Christ. This conversation didn't decrease the community's concern for the injustice that was facing black Americans; it widened their heart of concern.

Multiethnic witnessing communities are marked by people and leaders who are quick to listen to their community, prayerfully listen to the Holy Spirit for direction, courageously admit their blind spots and mistakes, and willingly change to make space for more people.

Instead of being a threat that leads to division, conflict becomes an opportunity for deeper reconciliation, shalom, and kingdom witness.

QUESTIONS FOR INDIVIDUAL REFLECTION AND SMALL GROUP DISCUSSION

1. What is the most striking thing you noticed about the response of the apostles in Acts 6:1-7?

2. What's your default response in crosscultural conflict?

3. What's the most challenging thing about the recommended steps to responding in crosscultural conflict?

4. For ministry leaders: What is the ethnic composition of your leadership team? How does it compare to your community and/or who you intend to reach? What critical voices and perspectives are missing from your team? Who could you invite to serve as an advisor or as a new leader?

RECOMMENDED READING

Churches, Culture and Leadership: A Practical Theology of Congregations and Ethnicities by Mark Lau Branson and Juan F. Martinez

Cross-Cultural Conflict: Building Relationships for Effective Ministry by Duane Elmer

Difficult Conversations: How to Discuss What Matters Most by Douglas Stone, Bruce Patton, and Shelia Heen

Divided by Faith: Evangelical Religion and the Problem of Race in America by Michael O. Emerson and Christian Smith

9

PROPHETIC
ETHNIC JUSTICE

What is justice? Justice appeals to one's sense of fairness and is about setting things right. Justice recognizes wrong and tries to correct, stop, compensate, and punish in order to right the wrong. Justice can be pursued in many arenas. Environmental justice looks at practices that are destroying ecosystems, and the response of "That's not right!" leads to petitions, policy changes, penalties for polluting companies, and necessary reforms. Gender justice looks at the abusive and unequal treatment of women, and the response of "That's not right!" seeks to put abusers behind bars, provides educational and vocational opportunities to women, and empowers and protects their rights. Justice in the context of the worldwide poor looks at child slavery and prostitution (among other issues), and the response of "That's not right!" seeks to break the cycles of poverty by providing access to clean water, housing, jobs, and education so that the world's most vulnerable will not fall prey to prostitution, beggary, child slavery, or parasitic moneylenders.

The pursuit of justice can be about the redistribution of goods (distributive justice), punishing the wrong (retributive justice), or about the fair processes and treatment in legal and organizational settings (procedural justice), as well as other models.

This book focuses particularly on ethnic justice in the United States. We are addressing what it means to be people of God who intentionally confront injustice that targets ethnic-specific and racially-specific groups of people. And who we are, ethnically, matters. People should speak out about issues that affect their own ethnic community, just as the black church has done in its rich history. But we are also called to speak out against injustices that affect those whose ethnicity differs from ours.

Returning to the image of Kintsukuroi pottery, imagine that you are a cup among many cups in a cupboard. You notice that the vases in the cupboard are beautiful, with many gleaming seams of gold in their former cracks. But as you get to know them better, they mention that something is hitting them, and more cracks appear. What is the loving thing to do? You could assume that this doesn't affect you because you are a cup, and the vases will take care of it on their own. But this is unloving! We are called to care for each other and learn about the cracks that are causing harm to ethnically specific communities. Dr. Martin Luther King Jr., who was obviously keenly aware of the injustices affecting his black community, displayed a similar awareness of the plight of his white neighbors: "I saw how the systems of segregation ended up in the exploitation of the Negro as well as the poor whites. I grew up deeply conscious of the varieties of injustice in our society."[1]

Resources on Justice Issues

The Little Book of Restorative Justice by Howard Zehr
A People's History of the United States by Howard Zinn
Rich Christians in an Age of Hunger by Ronald J. Sider
Social Justice Handbook: Small Steps for a Better World by Mae Elise Cannon

FEARS IN ADDRESSING JUSTICE

For some Christian readers, seeing the word *justice* can raise suspicion that a secular liberal agenda has worked its way inappropriately into conversation about a life of faith in Jesus. For others, the fact that this chapter comes so late in the book may bother you.

To the first group, I say this: justice was never a notion that was separated from God's plans for his people. He rescued them from slavery in Egypt, and the story of his divine intervention formed the bedrock of how they were to understand their relationship of faith with him. They were to have a countercultural code of ethics, the Ten Commandments, which stood in opposition to the competitive, polygamous, cutthroat way of living that was the Canaanite norm. In addition, the Israelites were given careful instructions about defending the cause of widows and orphans, welcoming the foreigner, and caring for the poor. They were to rest on the Sabbath day, which provided relief for all, including the poor, and also displayed their trust in the God who provides. This would be true of the Sabbath year (year seven) and the year of Jubilee (year forty-nine) in which all debts would be absolved; people would receive back the property they previously sold and those who had been sold into slavery would have their freedom restored. Israel was to embody God's heart in how it treated women, children, slaves, and foreigners.

But Israel fails to do this, and God does not mince words in expressing his anger at not just Israel's idolatry but also the unjust practices that come out of their idolatry. Amos, Isaiah, Jeremiah, and other prophets speak about God's discontent and refusal to tolerate Israel's injustice and inhospitality toward the poor and foreigners. Israel is sent into exile because it failed to live as the people of the covenant. Even so, the prophet Ezekiel writes this promise from the God who will not give up on his people:

> For I will take you out of the nations; I will gather you from all the countries and bring you back into your own land. I will sprinkle clean water on you, and you will be clean; I will cleanse you from all your impurities and from all your idols. I will give you a new heart and put a new spirit in you; I will remove from you your heart of stone and give you a heart of flesh. And I will put my Spirit in you and move you to follow my decrees and be careful to keep my laws (Ezekiel 36:24-27)

Ezekiel is anticipating the coming of Jesus and the new life he gives to us when he dies on the cross. In Matthew 5:17, Jesus says, "I have not come to abolish [the Law or the Prophets] but to fulfill them." We cannot live the life God meant for us without the cross, resurrection, and indwelling presence of the Holy Spirit.

We must remember that abolitionism and the women's suffrage moment were primarily led by Christians with Biblical convictions. But given the current church's suspicion of the increasingly secular and liberal world, it has backed away from many of the justice movements it started. Though the word *dikaiosune* can be translated as either righteousness or justice, our emphasis on personal piety makes us underappreciate the corporate, justice-related aspects of righteousness.[2]

To the second group of disgruntled readers, the chapter on justice appears later in the book because our understanding and practice of justice must be built on the awareness of our ethnic self and accompanied by trust-building, crosscultural, and conflict resolution skills. Otherwise, the colorblind person may walk into a conversation about justice and make crosscultural mistakes. They may lack the ability to resolve conflict with their brothers and sisters. Justice comes later in the book not because it's unimportant but because it requires building blocks in order to be sustained. We can't seek justice if we aren't people of perseverance and reconciliation.

NAMING ETHNIC INJUSTICE

Although the United States is called the land of the free and the home of the brave, we must acknowledge that our country was built on the removal of Native Americans from their land and the enslavement of black people, who were constitutionally mandated in 1787 to count as only three-fifths of the white population for purposes of representation in Congress. The United States was founded with built-in laws of systemic injustice.

Some may say, "That was more than two hundred and forty years ago! Can't we get past it?" But those people forget that the Civil

Rights movement and the Voting Rights Act of 1965 are fairly recent events in our nation's history. People of color have had voting rights for only the last fifty-plus years.

But voting rights alone do not guarantee a just society. Systemic injustice is a part of our country's history, affecting housing regulations, educational opportunities, and the criminal justice system. Let's take a look at the fictional characters of Tim and John, who both enlisted in World War II to serve as soldiers. Tim is white, and John is black. Both fought courageously and returned home with medals and honors. Both were promised housing and education as compensation for their years of service.

Tim moves into a house in the suburbs with the help of a large government subsidy. He gets married, has two kids, a dog, and a white picket fence. Tim's house accrues value over the years. He finds a good job and is able to save enough to send his children and grandchildren to school.

John is a law-abiding, upstanding American citizen and decorated veteran with a wife, two kids, a dog, and a white picket fence, just like Tim. But he's blocked from moving into certain neighborhoods that seem to be majority white. He's able to find a house, but the Homeowners Refinancing Act of 1933 and the Federal Housing Act of 1934[3] specify that neighborhoods with colored occupants, particularly black and Mexican, are "high-risk" and in decline. As stated in PBS's *Race, the Power of an Illusion,*

> Real estate practices and federal government regulations directed government-guaranteed loans to white homeowners and kept non-whites out, allowing those once previously considered "not quite white" to blend together and reap the advantages of whiteness, including the accumulation of equity and wealth as their homes increased in value. Those on the other side of the color line were denied the same opportunities for asset accumulation and upward mobility.[4]

This practice of redlining certain neighborhoods means companies refuse to give mortgages, insurance, and other goods and services to such areas, which interferes with how much money John's house will be worth in the future. Without rising equity, his home is doomed to a perpetually low value when compared to Tim's. Then a decade later, as city and state officials are planning to build low-income housing projects, John's neighborhood is selected as the building site because it is already lower in land value. This affects the quality of the public education system, among other things, and many residents leave.

Fifty years later, John's house is worth one-eighth[5] of Tim's, though they both have worked hard to provide for their families. While Tim's grandchildren are able to attend college just fine, John's grandchildren have to take out loans for college and get nervous when thinking about accruing more debt.

When we talk about systemic injustice, we are talking about situations like John's. Though he tries his best, he is significantly less well off than Tim. Though he makes similar choices to Tim's, unfair policies and systems make it impossible for John to enjoy the same kind of safety, prosperity, and standard of living that is available to Tim. This in turn affects John's children, and John's children's children. We can see that something is wrong with the system when we realize that this is the experience of many black Americans.

The United States was built on unjust systems and laws that contributed to the prosperity of whites at the expense of the freedom and fair treatment of black and Native Americans. Subsequent laws made cheap immigrant labor possible but didn't offer protection or financial stability for Asian, Latino, or Eastern European immigrants. The unjust systems that continue to affect different communities of color today, including the historically poor white communities in Appalachian America, are linked to the unfair laws and ethnic prejudice of the past.

In order to contribute to ethnic justice, we must look beyond helping the poor by simply distributing goods and services. We must also examine the systems and biases that create and maintain poverty in ethnic communities. We must ask, what needs to change, and where is power being unjustly wielded to the detriment of a community? And how can we go about making it right by establishing laws and systems that benefit not just one ethnic group but all Americans?

JESUS' FIRST SERMON ABOUT JUSTICE

Jesus was born to a people who were no strangers to ethnic injustice. They had been conquered by four different empires over six to seven centuries. Each new empire was worse than the last. When the Greeks came into power, they tried to ridicule, demean, and supplant Jewish culture and customs. Uprising attempts were ruthlessly met, often with crucifixion. Hasmonean King Alexander crucified eight hundred Jewish men "in the sight of all the city" who had attempted to revolt (Josephus, *Ant.* 13:380-1). Before they died, their wives and children were killed in front of them. Public mass crucifixions continued in Rome-occupied Israel (see Josephus, *Ant.* 12:256, 17:295, and Josephus, *War* 2:241, 5:449-51). It was a warning: do not try to fight Rome and the powers that be. The cross was a reminder that someone else was in power—someone that disregarded the value of Jewish life and saw it as expendable. The irony of the *Pax Romana* (Roman Peace) is that peace was established by the decimation and destruction of the people Rome conquered.

This is the troubled arena Jesus enters. At the beginning of his teaching years, he goes to the synagogue in Nazareth and reads this passage from the book of Isaiah:

> "The Spirit of the Lord is on me,
>> because he has anointed me
>> to proclaim good news to the poor.
> He has sent me to proclaim freedom for the prisoners
>> and recovery of sight for the blind,

to set the oppressed free,
to proclaim the year of the Lord's favor."

Then he rolled up the scroll, gave it back to the attendant and sat down. The eyes of everyone in the synagogue were fastened on him. He began by saying to them, "Today this scripture is fulfilled in your hearing." (Luke 4:18-21)

What a proclamation of hope, a vision of release for prisoners, and freedom for the oppressed! Jesus' first sermon emphasizes his commitment to justice as he proclaims the kingdom of God.

But the story doesn't end there. When the crowd questions Jesus, he shares with them a most unexpected story. He reminds them that throughout Israel's history, God chose to include and involve non-Jews—Gentiles—in his story. God provided for a widow in Sidon and cleansed the skin disease of the Syrian general Naaman, an oppressor of Israel's people.

These stories upset the Jewish listeners, and they try to kill him:

All the people in the synagogue were furious when they heard this. They got up, drove him out of the town, and took him to the brow of the hill on which the town was built, in order to throw him off the cliff. But he walked right through the crowd and went on his way. (Luke 4:28-30)

To imply that God's story of salvation might possibly include their ethnic enemies may have felt like pouring salt into an open, bleeding wound for these oppressed people. To then be told to love their enemies, who most certainly included Roman soldiers and Samaritans, probably felt inconceivable. And yet this seems to also be part of Jesus' inaugural sermon.

Jesus' kingdom message seems to simultaneously include freedom for the oppressed *and* the inclusion of the ethnic enemy, the oppressor. Indeed, later he welcomes and heals Roman centurions, despised tax collectors, and those who represented ethnic enemies such as the Samaritans and Greeks. What kind of justice is this?

PROPHETIC, RESTORATIVE ETHNIC JUSTICE

The Jewish listeners, who were deeply rooted in oral tradition, would have known the next part of Isaiah 61: after "to proclaim the year of the LORD's favor" is "and the day of vengeance of our God" (Isaiah 61:2).

Vengeance may have sounded sweet to the Jews. But I don't think that retributive justice fully encompasses what Jesus is declaring.

In the days following the Rwandan 1994 genocide, the country lacked the courts, jails, and resources to pursue procedural and retributive justice for everyone who had committed crimes. They instead turned to restorative justice, restoring relationships between perpetrators and victims, in hopes of stopping the cycles of ethnic cleansing that had plagued Rwanda's history.

In Luke 19, Jesus chooses to dine with Zacchaeus, who is a chief tax collector and thus gained much by collecting highly inflated taxes from his own countrymen on behalf of Rome. He is considered a traitor by his people, who mutter against Jesus' choice to visit his house. Zacchaeus' response to Jesus is astounding: "Here and now I give half of my possessions to the poor, and if I have cheated anybody out of anything, I will pay back four times the amount" (Luke 19:8). Zacchaeus has a real change of heart as a result of his encounter with Jesus, and he seeks both to distribute his wealth to the poor and also do right by those he wronged by quadrupling the amount he cheated out of them. It's extraordinary and costly.

Jesus' justice is restorative. In Jesus' economy, relationship is the highest currency because our relationships with each other reflect the divine image of the Trinity. All justice is focused on restoration of relationship, which means caring for others as if they are our own flesh and blood. We are created for communion with God and each other, and in the last days, we will enjoy fellowship with the triune God and his people. As a result, restorative justice is inherently communal. According to N. T. Wright,

> God's justice is a saving, healing, restorative justice, because the God to whom justice belongs is the Creator God who has yet to complete his original plan for creation and whose justice is designed not simply to restore balance to a world out of kilter but to bring to glorious completion and fruition the creation, teeming with life and possibility, that he made in the first place. And he remains implacably determined to complete this project through his image-bearing human creatures and, more specifically, through the family of Abraham.[6]

The Good Samaritan story challenges us to love strangers and ethnic enemies as our own, not in one moment, but for the long haul. It invites us to view the ethnic other as a beloved brother or sister. And what wouldn't you do for your family?

- Wouldn't you seek to make sure that they have all that they need, not just to survive, but to flourish?

- Wouldn't you seek to make sure that they are protected from their offenders, that those who caused harm are prevented from doing so again, and help to establish laws where all could be safe?

- If your brother or sister were the offender, wouldn't you do all in your power to help them repent and change for the better in order to have a second chance at life?

Jesus' restorative justice is reconciling. It unites the powerful with the oppressed, the offender with the victim, and the establishment with the foreigner. Restorative justice requires confession and agreement upon the injustice, inequity, and grievance involved. It requires the rejection of self-preservation on both sides: the right to harbor resentment toward the offender and the right to self-protect through wealth, power, and denial. It requires deep sacrifice of both. It's unfair and abusive to tell the victim or oppressed to choose grace and forgiveness while requiring no heart change of the powerful or the offender. In *Roadmap to Reconciliation*, Brenda Salter McNeil writes, "Reconciliation is an ongoing spiritual process involving forgiveness, repentance and justice that restores broken relationships and systems to reflect God's original intention for all creation to flourish."[7]

In the debate about racial reparations to black Americans, there is a valid concern about why the US government agreed to apologize and provide financial compensation to Native Americans for taking their lands and to Japanese Americans sent to internment camps during World War II, while black American descendants of slaves and those affected by Jim Crow laws have not been compensated.[8] This question must continue to be discussed in matters of US policy. However, reparations will not restore relationship. It will compensate but not heal what is broken. An example of reparative justice would be forcing the affluent great-grandson of a white slave owner to pay higher taxes so that reparations can be paid to the grandson of the slave his great-grandfather owned. It would be forced, begrudging, and likely to breed more political fractures. However, restorative justice in this example would be pursued at a communal level. The great-grandson of the white slave owner (who may or may not be called to pay those higher taxes) would say to the black grandson, "Would you become my family? Your nephews, nieces, and children will become part of my life. I will help you make sure that they will be able to graduate school and go to college so that they have access to the opportunities needed to flourish. Come be my family. Come vacation with us, dine with us. Teach me how to love you. Let us be one." The church should be praying and seeking such restoration of relationships and seeking the holistic physical, financial, and spiritual well-being of the other, especially because it possesses the good news of Christ and the power of the Holy Spirit, which can bring about deep loving of the other.

Justice and mercy are the twin hearts of God's righteousness. The community that is called to justice in Jesus' name is called to both, as merciless justice treats people as unredeemable, while unjust mercy pardons wrongs with no consequence and does little to challenge and dismantle injustice.

Today, we see what happens when people are treated as unredeemable in our criminal justice system. Young people come out of prison even more hardened than when they first entered. Young boys who committed foolish mistakes become fossilized in their ways because prisons don't provide the family, mentorship, or community they need. Yes, we should provide consequences for crimes in order to create a safe society but not at the cost of giving up on those who could be restored to a flourishing life.

Jesus' restorative justice is prophetic. Justice that exposes injustice communicates God's intolerance for oppression. But Jesus' justice isn't just about fixing what is wrong here on earth. It's about declaring the kingdom of God. Isaiah 61 paints a picture about the oppressed being freed, the prisoners being released, and the days of mourning and despair being replaced by praise and joy. It's a picture of restoration that anticipates the final resurrection when Jesus will come back and wipe the tears from our eyes.

Every time we care for an ethnic stranger, advocate for reform in our criminal justice system, stand up for refugees and immigrants, forgive our ethnic enemies, repent of sin against ethnic others, and give of ourselves, we are declaring the kingdom of God in ways that are compelling and undeniable. The kingdom of God is here and not yet. How we love each other and give of ourselves offers others a glimpse of the final resurrection that is coming. When we pursue restorative justice and proclaim Jesus at the heart of it, we serve as heralds of that final resurrection. Pursuit of justice declares that there is a king, whose rule and laws must be obeyed, and that he will overthrow all other kingdoms. We cannot achieve full justice on this side of heaven, but we can prepare for the coming of the one who will make things right. Restorative justice in Jesus' name proclaims that the hope of the good news is at the center of why we care for the poor, fight injustice, forgive enemies, and give our time, money, and energy for the other.

ASK JESUS TO OPEN YOUR EYES TO INJUSTICE

So how do we go about pursuing prophetic, restorative, and kingdom-declaring ethnic justice?

The first step is to open our eyes. And since we're talking about doing this as Jesus followers, we're going to ask Jesus to open our eyes to the ethnic injustice around us.

In John 2, Jesus exposes the injustice in the temple courts. During this time, temple and Roman taxes likely combined for a 30 to 40 percent tax rate, which fell heavily on the backs of the poor.[9] Plus, Jews had to change their money into acceptable currency at exorbitant interest rates, which benefitted the moneychangers at the temple.[10] Given these conditions, the poor in particular would have problems engaging in temple worship. Jesus sees this and is moved to anger. He flips the tables over and drives the moneychangers out of the temple. To those selling doves, the offering that the poorest worshipers could afford, Jesus says, "Get these out of here! Stop turning my Father's house into a market!" (John 2:16). This isn't a catatonic, lamb-holding Jesus. This is a Jesus who can't stand injustice and directly exposes it.

Likewise, we need to ask Jesus to open our eyes. The recent rise of the Black Lives Matter movement brought to light a pattern of injustices that affect the black American community in the United States, particularly the disparity in the use of force against unarmed black men, women, and children. The lack of indictment in those cases raises further outcry that something is wrong with the criminal justice system. Today we have more black Americans in prisons or jail and on

probation or parole than the total number of people that were enslaved in 1850, a decade before the Civil War.[11] Because going to
prison removes one's right to vote as well as the chances at procuring
stable employment, we have a vast majority of black Americans caught
in a kind of indentured servitude. Having a black president didn't
remove the problem of racial injustice. If anything, the fact that some
of these issues came to light during the years of his presidency shows
that these systems are difficult to overcome.

Jesus may open your eyes by inviting you to read books such as *The
New Jim Crow* by Michelle Alexander or *America's Original Sin* by
Jim Wallis. Jesus may open your eyes through the stories of friends
and colleagues that address issues you've never talked about before. I
have lived between Harvard University and the Massachusetts Institute of Technology for the past sixteen years. And every black
American man I've met knows that his doctorate degree or clerical
collar doesn't protect him from random stops by police and subtle
everyday racism. Education and enlightenment are no protection
against racial prejudice.

It's essential for your eyes to be opened to patterns of ethnic injustice in your own country. Because if you are unaware and then enter
a different context, you will bring the following problems: you could
carry over your unconscious biases and practices of injustice toward
ethnic others, you might not be able to understand the ethnic injustices
present in that context, or you may perpetuate the systems of ethnic
injustice found in the community you are trying to love and help.

LISTEN TO THE STORIES,
RECOGNIZE THE PATTERNS

If you find people who are willing to share their experiences of enduring racism with you, listen with care and respect. Don't react by
trying to play the devil's advocate or rationalizing the other side. Understand that the person is already hurting and taking a risk by sharing

with you. Particularly if there are tears, receive them as sacred and listen with care.

It's surprising when people share their concerns and opinions with me about Black Lives Matter without ever having learned about their core values, which include nonviolence. And while it's true that some Black Lives Matters protesters unfortunately deviate from that value, don't judge the movement by the outliers. Listen to what key people are saying before forming your opinion. Even if you don't feel comfortable supporting the movement after you have spent time learning, if you aren't concerned enough to ask about alternate ways you can be fighting the injustices highlighted by the movement, you haven't really been listening to the stories.

Listening to the pain of the black community illuminates the ethnic injustices faced by other communities. It helps us see what we previously could not. If we refuse to acknowledge the police brutality affecting black people, it's difficult to recognize police brutality and prejudice involved in the deaths of young, unarmed Latino American men. It's difficult to recognize the injustices faced by the Native American community, which we sometimes overlook due to its smaller size and lesser-known presence.

The 2016 Academy Awards for movies faced a backlash dubbed #OscarsSoWhite because the major award categories included only white nominees. Chris Rock, a black comedian, served as the emcee and provided helpful insights through some pointed jokes and comments. But he also told some tasteless and stereotyping jokes aimed at Asian Americans. Actor Sacha Baron Cohen, dressed as his Ali G character, added more racist comments. It seemed as though Hollywood was trying to fix its racism problem by hiring a black emcee and directing racist comments toward a different people group—hardly a corrective. After the broadcast, a Chinese American administrator at an urban charter school said sadly to me, "I have spent most of my life advocating for the education and rights of my black brothers and sisters. After the Oscars, I found myself wondering, would they do the same for me?"

I'm grateful for the many black colleagues and friends who voiced objection to the Oscars because of its racist jokes aimed at Asian Americans. Many of them had taken the time to learn the Asian American story and recognized that the Oscars are just one of many systems in which Asian Americans have to fight to be represented, respected, and seen as truly American.

My pastor, Dave, and his wife, Michelle, are both white, and they have eleven adopted children from around the world. When they adopted a trio of teenagers from Uganda, there were many things that Dave learned the hard way. When their son Robert got his driver's license, he was frequently pulled over or followed at random by the police. One day, Robert got rear-ended by a middle-aged white woman. When Robert asked Dave what to do, Dave confidently told him to call the police. Dave drove out to meet his son on the highway, and he was surprised and outraged to find that the police officer had dismissed the white woman and was instead giving a ticket to Robert! When Dave later shared the story with a group, the response of black parents was loud and clear: "What were you thinking, telling him to call the cops? Didn't you know any better?" Dave was taken aback. For him, you called the police for help. For the black people in his congregation, the police represented untrustworthy trouble. Dave was forced to recognize that these patterns and stories affect his son.

From the pulpit, Dave challenged us to listen, learn, and care about the fact that patterns of injustice affect in particular our black and brown brothers and sisters. Hearing the stories of men and women whose ethnicities and experiences of injustice are so different from our own helped us recognize these patterns.

Believing the stories of those around us is the first step in the long journey of building trust and engaging in justice. We also need to learn stories and read literature about ethnic injustice as it relates to our communities, neighborhoods, schools, and workplaces.

Daisy, a Latina friend who studies US immigration issues, patiently and passionately explained to me the issues at work in immigration policy. Many Central Americans are fleeing from war and conflict-induced poverty, just like Africans from the Congo and Sudan or Asians from Vietnam or Laos. Her question is, what makes these groups worthy of refugee status in the United States while Central American migrants are viewed as unwanted and treated like criminals? What kind of biases form the policy decisions that open doors to some while closing doors to others? Daisy exposed a part of the system that I have yet to fully understand—a system that thrives on cheap, illegal labor but vilifies it at the same time. This new understanding now informs how I think about the mentoring needed for Latino youths to thrive in schools or the ELL (English Language Learner) and adult education classes needed for Latino adults.

PURSUE ETHNIC JUSTICE NOW

Once you are learning about others' stories and patterns, there are some concrete next steps to take in pursuit of justice.

Form a small group that prays and pursues justice together. Whether it's a small group that reads this book together, a prayer group, or a discussion group, create a space where people can share their stories and concerns and then pray about next steps. Use the crosscultural communication skills mentioned in the previous chapters as you interact with each other. Continue learning together by reading a book, attending a lecture, learning from a community organizer, or starting a sermon series that focuses on justice and reconciliation. Make space to pray for local and national incidents related to race and ethnicity.

Connect with a local group that is committed to pursuing justice, advocacy, or activism (faith-based or secular). Consider finding out more about the local Black Student Union on campus or the American

Civil Liberties Union office in your town. Or try a community non-profit, youth-mentoring program, justice-oriented mentoring program, or prison ministry program at a church. Look for groups with clear goals and a stated mission such as Campaign Zero, which has concrete objectives that include limiting unhelpful police interventions, improving community interactions, and ensuring accountability. There are leaders who are already experts in what they know and practice. Learn from them. Watch how they navigate systems and call for public accountability from civil servants. Pray for them.

Partner with local ethnic-specific churches that are attuned to the needs of their ethnic community. Latino, black, and Asian American churches that are established in a city are more likely to know the poverty, justice, and immigration issues affecting their community. They might have ELL classes or food pantries, youth mentoring programs, and existing relationships with the city and cross-church partnerships you could join.

Stay involved in the civic arena. Vote. Whether you're Republican, Democrat, Independent, or other, advocate for justice. Raise the issues, because justice is something that concerns us all. Write to your congressional representatives about issues of injustice that you want them to address. Pay attention to what is being said by candidates in local and national elections. Call them to accountability through letters, petitions, and your vote.

Show up when a community is in pain. If there's a race-related incident locally or nationally, show up for the prayer vigils, the nonviolent protests, and the community meetings. Ask how you can be praying for and caring for the affected community.

After the terrorist attacks on 9/11, my Asian American college fellowship sent a letter to the Muslim Student Association on campus, writing that we knew from experience what it was like to represent the face of the enemy at war (specifically, the Japanese Americans who were sent to internment camps during World War II). The letter asked how we could be praying for them. We heard nothing for several months. Then in December, two women wearing headscarves attended our fellowship meeting. They quietly and respectfully sat in the back and asked to speak during our announcements. "We got your letter. Thank you," they said. "And it has been very hard. Please continue to pray for us. We are grateful for you because you are the only group that reached out to us." This started a relationship that lasted for the next ten years. We built trust with members of the Muslim Student Association community by studying the Scripture and the Koran together, sharing Ramadan dinners, and talking about spiritual matters. Our response during the crisis cemented trust for the next decade; what we do now builds trust for a lifetime.

PURSUE ETHNIC JUSTICE FOR A LIFETIME

Pursuing justice isn't just a phase of life. It's a way of life, and you're invited to a lifelong journey of seeking justice and loving your neighbor. Whether you're a teacher, lawyer, policymaker, active parent in the PTA, or doctor, issues of racial bias and ethnic injustice affect the people you work with, serve, lead, and live among. Check with a neighbor or a fellow parent in your community when an incident affects their ethnic community. Stay informed of the evolving issues and news that affect your work and neighborhood. Find other people in your work and region that have similar values. Talk to your kids at an early age about how they can stand up to racial bullying (and bullying in general), and teach them to value ethnic difference as a beautiful thing. Consider working on projects or serving communities that experience a disproportionate amount of ethnic injustice so that you can prayerfully work toward change in that arena. Serve as a Big Brother or Sister to someone who is ethnically different than you or help teach an ELL class. Explore foster care. Advocate not just for diversity in the workplace or school but also for skills and ethnicity training that can help those spaces decrease in racism and bias. Pay attention to what bills are being proposed, and write, call, or email to petition your representatives and hold them accountable.

QUESTIONS FOR INDIVIDUAL REFLECTION AND SMALL GROUP DISCUSSION

1. Name a time when your eyes were opened to ethnic injustice. What was the event or experience that helped you do that?
2. What is a pattern of ethnic injustice that concerns you? What are some next steps you can take to address that concern?
3. What's a next step for you individually and corporately?
4. Who are some local organizations or people that you can connect with in order to learn more?
5. What are some fears or questions that come up for you about engaging in ethnic justice?

RECOMMENDED READING

Evil and the Justice of God by N. T. Wright

Just Spirituality: How Faith Practices Fuel Social Action by Mae Elise Cannon

Pursuing Justice: The Call to Live and Die for Bigger Things by Ken Wytsma with D. R. Jacobsen

Roadmap to Reconciliation: Moving Communities into Unity, Wholeness and Justice by Brenda Salter McNeil

Stride Toward Freedom by Martin Luther King Jr.

Welcoming Justice: God's Movement Toward Beloved Community by Charles March and John M. Perkins

Welcoming the Stranger by Matthew Soerens and Jenny H. Yang

10

CULTURE
RE-CREATORS

My friend Hilary helps lead an annual ceremony of blessing for the Native American students she works with. After listening to different Native speakers describe their journeys of healing cultural trauma and receiving an invitation to embrace the way our Creator made them Native, students are given blankets that are wrapped around them by a minister and elders as a symbol of blessing. When asked how that was received, given that "gifts" of smallpox-infested blankets had been used to decimate the Native people, Hilary replied, "We're pretty up front in acknowledging what blankets have represented in the past for Native people. But instead of using it to curse, we're using it to bless. As we pray over them and celebrate who they are, we are redeeming the meaning of the blankets. The students think it's pretty cool, and a lot of them have described the 'blanket ceremony' as their favorite thing about that gathering."

Jesus' people also faced the potential wiping out of their people and story. But Jesus acted as a culture re-creator, a maker of new culture, as he invited his people and others into redemption. Jesus did not come to dismantle Jewishness. He came to help the Jewish people become fully Jewish. The Jews were liberated from Egypt in order to be a priesthood nation to all of their neighbors. But without the Holy Spirit writing the law on their hearts, they could not. Once they were sent to be disciplemakers of every nation, they were invited to be the priesthood people. Paul, the rabidly ethnocentric Pharisee supremacist, became the unlikely carrier of the gospel to all nations. He thought he was embodying what it meant to be a true Israelite, but he could not do so without Jesus. Instead of being a culture preserver or destroyer (and indeed, he was very destructive before meeting Jesus), Paul was invited to become a re-creator, a culture-maker in Jesus' name.

My friend worked at a Covenant church named Jesus the Re-creator, and I can't think of a better way to name what Jesus does at the cross and through his resurrection. The cross marks Jesus' defeat of death and sin and heralds his eventual defeat over all death in the world to come. The broken world is being re-created by a good healer and redeemer as he invites us into his work of re-creating our culture.

As we talk about ethnicity, we're not just talking about remembering cultural heritage. We're talking about creating new culture that builds off of ethnic history and knowledge and, in Jesus' name, helps create something new that blesses the nations and helps others come to know him. Creating new culture means having a powerful and relevant impact on the arts, on justice, in the thought world, and in society as whole. And new culture pays homage to the roots from which it came, recognizing both the good and the bad.

When we are ethnically aware of our beauty and scars, and when we are aware of the *imago Dei* and pain in others, we have the opportunity to be culture re-creators, much like the early church that saved the dying and orphaned babies during the plagues and much like Martin Luther King Jr. and all those who marched for freedom. When Christians are divorced from understanding their secular context, they become ineffective and exclusive communities that have no real impact on the world around them. Andy Crouch, author of *Culture Making*, calls the church to move beyond condemning, critiquing, copying, or consuming culture.[1] He writes that culture is not just simply how we think; it is what we make of the world. And he invites Christians to become culture makers.

Being ethnically aware helps us re-create culture without dismissing the past. It helps us avoid appropriating the stories of others because the ethnically aware self aims to be cognizant of beauty and brokenness, scars and tears, in its learning of all stories. And it helps us avoid wandering as houseless vagabonds who keep searching for home in the stories of others while avoiding being in touch with our own roots. Culture re-creation honors heritage.

UNEXPECTED CULTURE RE-CREATING

In 2001, a young rapper faced off against Hassan, the reigning champion of the Freestyle Friday rap battle competition on Black Entertainment Television (BET). Hassan had won six victories and was on his way to BET's hall of fame.

His opponent was MC Jin, a nineteen-year-old Chinese American who filled thirty seconds with confident rhymes and unabashed references to his ethnicity, including telling Hassan, "If you make one joke about rice or karate, NYPD be in Chinatown searchin' for your body."

Hassan gave up with more than fifteen seconds left after delivering some limp lines about wontons and sexual inexperience, meant to poke fun at Jin's ethnic background. Jin stole the show, won six more battles, and landed in the BET hall of fame.

What was a Chinese American doing in an arena dominated by black Americans? Though Jin had a promising start because of the BET show, his first album in the United States flopped. He was guided by well-intentioned people who didn't know how to help a Chinese American break into a market with almost no other Asian Americans. Years went by and then he received an invitation to record and remake himself in Hong Kong. Jin became a celebrity in Asia and then became a Christian who helped lead other well-known celebrities in Hong Kong to faith.[2]

I grew up watching many Asian Americans gravitate toward hip-hop and rap, and I've heard Asian Americans lament and criticize that they lack their own distinct style of music: "Why can't we have our own? Why do we need to borrow or steal from black culture?"

To those critics, I'd say that for many Asian Americans, the expression of the black struggle, of not being white and being mistreated as a person of color, is something that resonates with Asian Americans. Especially for those who grew up as children of poor immigrants, rap music talks about the struggle of poverty and having a hard life, which provides connection in ways that are not available in other music genres. Plus, rap is in English, a language they can understand, as opposed to the disconnection they may have with their parents' mother tongue. To have a different language from your parents means that one cannot fully communicate one's struggles, emotions, or experiences. Rap music provides Asian Americans a way to describe experiences and emotions that may never be understood by their parents. I understand why they gravitate toward music rooted in centuries of a developed black consciousness. To deny them that connection is dangerously close to saying that they cannot be American. Hip-hop is American. They are Asian American.

CULTURE MAKING AS RECOVERING WHAT WE DO NOT KNOW

But there is a second reason why Asian Americans gravitate to rap, and it's more complicated. In many Asian cultures, rhythm, dancing, song, spoken word, and improvisation are a part of their arts and cultures, spanning back for more than one thousand years. Many Asian Americans are cut off from understanding the language that is the backbone of these musical and artistic practices. Hip-hop was often the closest equivalent to the rhythm, drums, and dance that is a part of Chinese, Korean, Indian, and other Asian cultures. Perhaps without even knowing it, Asian Americans that gravitate toward hip-hop and rap are gravitating toward the closest equivalent to their ancestral heritage's artistic soul.

Missiologist Lamin Sanneh writes that language is a "living expression of culture" and that Christian mission helped "strengthen vernacular languages in their diverse particularity and enormous multiplicity."[3] Though missionaries often brought Western colonization, Sanneh notes that their insistence on translating the Bible into the local language helped preserve the culture, especially in cultures that had no written language. He contrasts this with Islam's spread in Africa. Islam has a central language (Arabic) with an accompanying centralized culture that replaces local culture and language. Sanneh argues that language is the preserver of culture. Think about the nuance and variety of vocabulary, slang, grammar, and accents in English (in different parts of the United States, in England, Ireland, Australia, etc.) or in the Spanish or French spoken all around the world. Spoken words contain so much of the culture.

My mother's side of the family is descended from a line of artists, philosophers, and senators who spoke up against the government and were banished. They are known for their artistic flair and musical ability. There is a Korean folk song titled "Arirang" that has a sweet pentatonic scale and peaceful rhythm. Every Korean province plays a slightly altered version. My mother's relatives turn it into a rhythmic, minor-scaled song full of flair, claps, and syncopation, sounding more like an old black American spiritual or a Native American song than the original.

When my mother's youngest sister got married, my grandparents gathered their village in Jindo, Jeolla Province, to celebrate. People drummed and sang, and after the chorus of "Arirang," each person made up their own rhyming lines of spoken word and song celebrating the marriage, expressing joy that all five of my grandparents' children were married, and wishing many grandchildren upon them. My father, who is not from that province, marveled and said afterward, "I understand now what they mean by the glory of Jindo's people."

Spoken word, drums, and rhythm are a deep part of my ethnic cultural heritage. Many Asian Americans don't know their cultural heritage because such knowledge is lost with language. When immigrant children come to a new country and try to survive and thrive, the price paid for their successful assimilation into American life is losing the language that binds them to their ancestral culture.

This is one of the gifts of the black community: the arts, particularly music, became the primary vehicles and carriers of their ethnic story—of resistance against slavery and racism, of remembering history, and pointing toward hope. Black Americans spent much of the past four centuries without power, and their songs captured their fight against injustice and stories of pain that white-dominated history books and stories could not. And it's in English. Black stories and culture are passed down in the same language, though in evolving musical forms. Black culture produces musical, artistic revolution amid their suffering. They refuse to let brokenness have the final say. They refuse to buy into a cheapened gospel.

The arts, and the arts particularly from the black American experience, have shaped culture in the United States, and music produced by the black community has profoundly shaped many American cultural revolutions. Awareness of ethnic story has been passed on from generation to generation. Awareness of its beauty and pain has allowed for the powerful creation of poetry, literature, spoken word, music, rap, and other art that often incorporates gospel hope into its notes and words. Contrast this with immigrant communities who don't share the same language or racial awareness that they could pass on to their children.

When I reflect on the version of "Arirang" from my mother's village and I hear its minor, rhythmic turns, I hear the sound of a people who were oppressed, who used the arts and words to protest and continue to use them—just like the black community in the United States. Hearing the old songs about hope and freedom from the black tradition helps me hear those notes of hope in the songs of my own people. I notice when it's present, and I notice when it's missing. Much of non-Christian Asian understanding of self is cyclical: life is suffering, and you will be reborn into another life, hopefully to suffer less. The Christian understanding of self is linear: this is the one life we have, and there is assurance of triumph at the end of God's story. What turned a tiny half-peninsula country such as Korea into the one of the largest missionary sending bases of the world?[4] Something about the story of the gospel tapped into the real awareness of pain and struggle of the Korean people and released it for a new story of sharing hope with the rest of the world.

RECOVERING ETHNIC CULTURE

Moses, who represents both the powerful and the oppressed as an adopted Egyptian prince of Hebrew origins, killed an Egyptian in order to protect the Hebrews. He was repudiating his Egyptian background. When the people he considered his own rejected him, Moses fled far away from both Egypt and Israel to Midian, repudiating his Jewishness. He sought to erase his past. But God had other plans for him. He wove together Moses' Hebrew heritage and his Egyptian upbringing as a prince to deliver the Israelites from slavery.

Left to our own devices, we can be like Moses. We can become destroyers of culture or reject our own people. We can consume or dismiss the ethnic culture of others. A colorblind society eager to run from the past can try to dismiss ethnic culture in many ways. But Jesus doesn't do that.

My friend Sherami, a German American from Iowa, talked with me about the difficulty of trying to recover the culture of the German heritage in her family. For many German Americans, it was tricky to be German during and after World War II. You represented the enemy and those who were responsible for the Holocaust. In order to show that you were a loyal American, many German-descended Americans stopped speaking German and tried to assimilate as much as possible to what they considered to be mainstream culture. Sherami's family was no exception.

In her campus ministry, Sherami has been helping white men and women enter into conversations about race and ethnicity. She encountered confusion, emotions, and defensiveness in her fellow white people. She asked me mournfully, "How do I recover what was not explicitly taught to me? How do I teach other people to learn what was never taught to them?" She wrestled with the poverty of knowledge, with how her family had been affected by the pressures to assimilate and as a result lost part of their ethnic story. This is not just an issue for her family or just German Americans. Many European immigrants lost the connection to their ethnic heritage stories in the forced or voluntary assimilation to whiteness.

We prayed that God would open doors for Sherami to recover the culture that was never passed down to her. A year later, a distant cousin sent her a recording of her grandfather's voice. As she sat listening to his accented immigrant voice, she wept. "His voice! That German accent, so unmistakable! I understand now why my aunts and uncles talk a certain way, say certain things," she said. Sherami connected with a part of her ethnic story that had been closed to her. As she learned about her grandfather's immigrant story, she discovered that he opposed Hitler's rhetoric. She began understanding her German American heritage and herself as a white woman in new ways. And she got an answer to her prayers as Jesus showed that he cared about her ethnic heritage.

Sherami is acquiring stories and experiences that will help her invite others into their own compelling journey to embrace their ethnic identity. This is especially important for white people because lack of self-knowledge in terms of ethnic history is a serious impediment for navigating multiethnic community.

We cannot help re-create culture if we do not know who we are or where we come from. With a deficit of self-knowledge, we don't have the building blocks necessary to create beauty, to honor the past, or to point to hope. We're at the mercy of those who know more or claim to know more, who can pick and choose and decide to tell us what to be.

In our nation's past, many Native Americans were tragically forced to give up their language and culture in the Christian boarding schools where Native children were sent after they were taken away from their parents. There is a growing awareness and movement to reclaim this lost Native culture. The body of Christ must be an important voice that affirms the embrace of Native history and culture. But the gospel won't be achieved by just reclaiming Native culture. We must also invite Native American Christians to be culture re-creators and makers who bring the beauty of their story and share the gospel through that lens.

Supaman is a Montana-based rapper descended from the Crow Nation. He is also a Christian who weaves references to faith and Jesus into his art. He performs as a dancer, rapper, and musician all over the world, and he often speaks to Native American youth about the value and beauty of their culture and heritage, which stands in stark contrast to how many Native youth view their ethnic selves. In a song called "Prayer Loop Song," he takes the tracks of old civil rights songs and overlays them with Native sounds and songs while rapping and borrowing from the hip-hop tradition that describes many realities of the inner city that parallel reservation life. Supaman is re-creating culture, paying homage to the old and telling the story of his people and of Jesus in a new way.

When we are rooted in our story, we become better receptacles of others' stories. Instead of culture destroyers, we become culture re-creators. We can make art that honors our stories and the stories of the other. Culture re-creation reveals the existing or hidden beauty in ourselves and in the other.

REMEMBERING INSTEAD OF APPROPRIATING

We need to remember and learn cultural and ethnic histories instead of resorting to shallow appropriation, in which people take or make use of something for one's own use, without authority or right.

For example, appropriation of Asian culture may include buying cultural artifacts such as a Chi-Pao gown, enjoying sushi or kimchi, learning a greeting in Chinese or Korean, or learning an Asian martial art, and then congratulating oneself as multicultural. But it's important to go deeper than that. We must take care in learning about the ethnic and provincial diversity of China and its people and take time to learn about the complexities, pain, and depth behind the immigrant stories of Asian Americans.

The celebration of Cinco de Mayo and St. Patrick's Day in the United States are other examples of cultural appropriation. These events are celebrated with drinking and the wearing of stereotyping costumes instead of with an understanding of their actual histories (Mexico's victory over France at the Battle of Puebla and the legacy of Saint Patrick, who served his former ethnic enemies as a spiritual leader).

In 2015, Annie Lennox, a white singer, was criticized for singing Billie Holiday's critically acclaimed song "Strange Fruit" because she refrained from explicitly discussing the song's significance in US history. The song is about lynching and how the South documented the violent act as if it were a sport; the "strange fruit" is the hanging bodies of black men, women, and children.

If we are unwilling to understand the history of something, then we can't do justice to its story. We end up appropriating, taking what is convenient. Appropriation is hurtful because it consumes the beauty of something without acknowledging, honoring, and addressing the pain. We use the N-word thinking it will make us cool or that we will gain more swagger, when we should be sensitive and aware of what the word has meant through our country's history. If we thought about it, we wouldn't use it. We can play music created by black artists because we like the rhythms or the beats without understanding the actual story behind the music. Consumerism lets us pick and choose what we want. We become gluttons of what feels good and deniers of pain and scars.

The beauty of the blues, soul, Motown, hip-hop, and rap music comes out when it's paying homage to history, crying out against suffering, and asking the existential and theological questions of "When will this end?" Spirituals were not just talking about heaven itself but also of the lands of promise on this side of heaven, where black men and women could be free before death came.

We can't understand the meaning behind the lyrics of black rapper Kendrick Lamar's "To Pimp a Butterfly" if we don't understand what the song is referencing—the appropriation of black culture, the execution and destruction of black Americans, the self-hatred that results, and also the breathtakingly beautiful life of blackness and black culture. If we love the music of black people and yet do little to care about the things they sing about, we fail to treat black Americans with care, honor, and respect.

The opposite of appropriation is homage and remembrance. Appropriation is partial, shallow savoring that destroys memory. Re-creation of culture remembers the beauty and the broken. Culture creation without homage to the past is appropriation of others' ethnic histories and the dismissal of our own. If we do not know our ethnic story, the past, we are rootless. You cannot find a home for yourself if you don't know the home from which you came. And you will certainly be a poor guest in the house of others. A wise Asian American colleague said to me once, "If we do not know who we are, we just end up taking from others."

AVOIDING CULTURAL FOSSILIZATION

Children of immigrants are usually told what it means to be their ethnic background. Their parents have very insistent perspectives on what it means to be Polish, Korean, or Chinese. But that definition is the way Poland, Korea, or China was when their parents left that country, sometimes decades ago—not the way it is now. Immigrants carry with them a time capsule impression from their parents of what it means to be their ethnicity, even though, of course, their hometowns and people change over time. Back in my parents' day in South Korea, most women married by age twenty-four. Nowadays, people don't get married until they are close to or older than thirty, and many women are choosing to be single because they wish to avoid the restrictions that might be placed onto them as daughters-in-law. It's a different world than the one my parents left in 1985.

Many churches, immigrant and not, hold on to traditions that are culturally normal for them. The conservative values of the previous generation don't necessarily appeal to the younger generations, and churches fail to change alongside our ever-evolving world. Churches that don't pay attention to changing cultural norms stand in danger of being inhospitable, irrelevant, and fossilized in a time capsule that no longer connects with the present day. Cultural preservation without theological reflection and challenge leads to fossilization. And fossilized churches become spaces that are defined by social gatherings instead of spaces to experience the real living presence of God.

CREATING NEW CULTURE IN SPIRITUAL AND BIOLOGICAL FAMILIES

As Christians, all of us are tasked with creating new spiritual families as we join with former strangers. Israel and later the church were invited to be a people of cultural re-creators, bringing life and bearing the image of God to those around them to form the new family of God. Likewise, as we form spiritual communities of support, love, and care, we are called to care for those outside our immediate family. We need to care for single people who are unmarried by choice or circumstance, as well as those who are going through the difficult pain of divorce. Every ethnic culture ostracizes such people; we can welcome their gifts, friendship, and presence. As mentors and friends of different ethnicities and life stages become dear parts of our lives, we learn more deeply how to love the other. Our spiritual families become radically hospitable and countercultural spaces as we grow in understanding ethnic beauty as well as witness together the healing from God.

My husband, Shin, was a youth group leader several years ago. We learned that two teenagers in his group were from families that had recently gone through difficult divorces. Wanting to give the parents a break from cooking, we invited them over for Shin's peach-whiskey-BBQ chicken on a Saturday night. The group included John, his mom, and his younger sister, who are black, and Anna, her younger sister (adopted Latina), and their white father. Given the mix of tweens, teens, and parents who didn't know each other too well, we thought it could be pretty awkward. We worried that they'd cancel when snow started to fall, but everyone came, bundled up against the cold. We had a great time, with my extroverted and artistic husband entertaining the party with YouTube videos of artists, dancers, and singers of every ethnic background. Everyone talked and shared, even the shyer tweens. We were a multiethnic, multi-life-stage group of people who stayed together in communion until almost midnight. One parent said it was a treat to not have to cook, while the other whispered to me that this was the first time he'd seen his daughter smile and laugh in a year. "Thank you," he said, giving us hugs.

After everyone left, my husband and I stood still, savoring the beauty of the night we'd just experienced. It's one of our favorite memories from our time in Boston. We felt like we had hosted angels. Jesus was expanding our understanding of community, and he continues to teach us how to be a spiritual family to married and single persons, divorcees and widows, to the parent overwhelmed by his kids or the couple struggling with infertility, across ethnic boundaries and differences.

As for creating new culture in biological families, there is no right formula. You could end up marrying someone of the same or different ethnic background, but what matters is how you live out your marriage as an ethnically aware couple. Those who think ethnic-specific marriages are the answer to preserving culture might be concerned about ethnic purity and conservancy. But that can lead to fossilizing and a lack of culture creation, which is needed to challenge idols and assumptions of norms in that culture. On the flip side, those who think mixed marriages are the only answer could be running away from or denying their ethnic histories instead of thoughtfully reflecting on who they are as ethnic people—beauty, complications, and all.

Both mixed-race marriages and marriages between people who share ethnic heritage are needed in an ethnicity-aware society and church community in order for us to understand our stories better and reconcile across differences. Ethnic-specific marriages can focus on bringing the best of their culture together to their community and explore regional variances in their shared ethnicity (my parents are both Korean, but they hail from two different provinces with different values). A white man with mostly German roots and a white woman with Irish and Norwegian roots can steward their whiteness together while sharing their different heritage stories and values with their spouse. A black woman married to a white man will together need to be intentional in recognizing the beauty as well as the scars in both sides so that they can address conflict in an ethnically aware manner and raise their children to honor both sides of the family. An Asian woman and a Latino man will marvel in the similarities as well as differences in how their cultures understand honoring their parents and creating a new family together. A family that adopts a child can help the child understand both her own ethnic heritage as well as the traditions of the family in which she is growing up.

MULTIRACIAL CHILDREN: OUR NEW CULTURE RE-CREATORS

The people who may most feel the tension and need of reconciliation in a diverse society are multiracial children. At a recent ministry conference, mixed-race people shared painful stories of being rejected by different sides of their communities. Domenic spoke about how the Italian side of his family would use ethnic slurs and say disparaging things about his Mexican mother's people. Whether on the playground or in his high school or college classroom, whenever he attempted to connect with Latinos, they rejected him because he could not speak Spanish. "I grew up hating who I was, on every side," he said. Others shared about navigating playgrounds, neighborhoods, and classrooms while being rejected by both of their sides or singled out as the other. One twenty-one-year-old man, both Haitian and Guatemalan, shared that the first time he had felt accepted was at a recent intentional dinner space for multiracial, multiethnic people. He had spent the first two decades of his life meandering from un-acceptance to confusion to isolation. These painful stories are not new. But hearing about the pain of multiracial people helped those who represented the different sides of those stories say to them, "We are sorry, brother. We love you, sister. You are part of our family."

These brothers and sisters hold the reality of different communities and ethnic stories living in one person. Our multiracial brothers and sisters have the difficult challenge of living out reconciliation and creating new culture every day as they navigate competing messages from different sides. But they may be the people to lead us in the repairing and restoring of broken connections between communities. Will we honor them as part of us while also encouraging them to seek the Lord in creating new culture? Our challenge is to say, "Look at the glory God put in you. Learn and own your story, and then teach me," instead of saying, "Well, we're all just human anyway."

Leah, who has a Polish mother and a father who is Puerto Rican and Italian, grew to embrace her Latino heritage after spending most of her childhood being rejected by Latinos because she didn't speak enough Spanish. In college, she was loved and encouraged to grow in her identity as a multiracial Latina. She read, prayed, and made space for Jesus to bring healing and wholeness to her journey. God grew her heart to reach out to Latinos who were not being reached by her college fellowship. Before her self-acceptance, she would have questioned her role and authority given her biracial heritage. But because she had experienced healing, she said yes to this call. She is now able to help both Latinos and multiracial persons own their stories because of the work God has done in her.

CULTURE RE-CREATION CENTERED ON HOPE

We need hope in order to be culture re-creators and re-shapers of society, justice, and reform. We need the Christian story of hope in order to write stories, paint masterpieces, and create musical scores that make us say yes to the home we long for. God's character and his story of hope in the cross and resurrection help us understand what is beautiful.

My husband and I are both artists. As part of an InterVarsity project, we created The Story Project, a large manga-style mural depicting stories of people being healed and restored by Jesus throughout the Scriptures: the man with leprosy, the blind man, the man possessed by Legion, the Samaritan woman at the well, the raising of Lazarus, and more (see http://2100.intervarsity.org/overview/story -project). The mural is six feet high and nine feet wide with brilliant colors and faces of every ethnicity. Jesus is depicted in six different ways: black, possibly Asian or Native, white, possibly Latino or Middle Eastern, wearing crowns of thorns, and breathing out living water. The mural was created to start spiritual conversations with people of every ethnicity and spiritual background. When we first tested it in Boston, students flocked to the mural—black Caribbean American women, young Latino students, white punk rockers with aqua-dyed blond hair, older Vietnamese American students, and Muslim Middle Eastern American women wearing headscarves. They were drawn to the colors and ethnic diversity of the mural, to the stories of people who looked like them. Young black students exclaimed, "There are people who look like me in this drawing!"

I met a woman who was an agnostic international student from Saudi Arabia. When I asked her what made her stop at the mural, she pointed at the ethnically diverse faces of Jesus. "I want to know why," she said.

As we shared the stories of Jesus bringing healing and restoration to the different characters, we also shared how Jesus brought healing and hope to our own stories, pointing to the stake in Jesus' wrist from which flows living water. We invited people to receive healing in places of brokenness and invited them to say yes to Jesus.

The Story Project has been used across the country and in sister organizations across the globe. We took pains to reflect the kingdom diversity each student group desired. When it was used by mostly white students in an artistic community, black students that had never before connected to the group approached the white leaders and asked, "What is this? Tell me about this drawing."

In his commencement address to Biola University students in 2012, Makoto Fujimura, a brilliant Japanese American abstract painter known for his use of traditional Japanese painting techniques, said the following:

> So today I ask you . . . "What do you want to make today?" It's a question posed to those leaving a school instead of being asked as you enter one. . . . Would you make today a future that is worth beholding? Will you choose to dedicate your days to creating a world that is worth passing onto your children?

Do not be washed away in apathy, entropy and decay. Instead of threatening the world with terrorism, and deny the fundamental endowed capacity to create in love, we need, in the quiet of your daily service, give sacrifice so that others may live. Art and love are fundamentally the same act, operating on the same sphere of our lives. You see, art is not a frivolous, peripheral activity, but it has to do with the deepest core of existence; it is to love yourself, and your neighbors. Art defines what makes us human; and fully human, we will be making things.[5]

WHAT DO YOU WANT TO MAKE TODAY?

We may not all be painters, but we all make things: friendships, families, cultures, careers, and memories. Each of us is called to create and re-create in that process.

In the summer of 2015, I gathered a multiethnic group of evangelistic InterVarsity staff from different parts of the country who ranged in age from twenty-three to forty. We explored and shared our ethnic stories, making space to reflect on how God made us well and also to lament and weep over how we were broken by sin. We studied the Scriptures and prayed blessings and forgiveness over one another. We washed one another's feet. In ethnically diverse pairs, we practiced preaching about how God brought healing to our ethnic stories and invited our listeners to follow Jesus the reconciler and become a Christian. We were commissioned to go and do preaching in pairs for the following year.

As each pair went out to preach, they started to see conversion, repentance, confession, healing, and new life. Native American students who heard that Jesus wanted to bless their culture and bring healing to the cracks in their stories said yes to Jesus. Andrew and Brent, respectively white and black Southerners, preached together and saw not only conversion but also healing and release from emotional bitterness, wounds, and spiritual oppression. As others incorporated ethnically aware teaching into their communities, they saw their leadership grow and change, their fellowships grow in diversity, and real reconciliation happen. They would speak up and speak out against injustice, host dinners for Muslim students, plant ministries to unreached ethnic groups, and help white students learn how they were created well and being restored in Jesus. Many of the stories you read in this book come from the experiences of those women and men. These experiences were changing us just as much as they were transforming our communities. We had front row seats to glory, even amid the rising racial tensions in the United States. And we are so grateful for a God whose story and message of hope makes this possible.

Hope can feel paltry and weak in a time when sin and brokenness seem to be normative in our world. But hope isn't a tool of the feeble-hearted. It's the food of those who have known suffering, who know the difference between comfort and yearning for the complete reversal of all things broken. Art without hope might be beautiful or intriguing or a nice mental exercise. But the stories, music, and paintings that tap into that place of hope in us hit a different chord. They are the most beloved of stories, like *The Lord of the Rings* or Harry Potter, and they help us live in hope.

Hope is what keeps us going. We, in our ethnic stories and selves, are called to live in hope and to pursue that hope. We live in the here and not yet. In the hope of the final resurrection, where God himself will wipe away every tear from every eye, we are called to proclaim the kingdom with all that we have. It is in doing so that we become culture re-creators.

QUESTIONS FOR INDIVIDUAL REFLECTION AND SMALL GROUP DISCUSSION

1. What are ways Jesus might be inviting you to remember your ethnic heritage?

2. How is Jesus inviting you to become a culture re-creator?

3. Where is Jesus inviting you to hope in how you practice community, reconciliation, crossing cultures, or justice?

4. What are some personal and communal next steps you can take after reading this book?

RECOMMENDED READING

The Beauty of God: Theology and the Arts edited by Daniel J. Treier, Mark Husbands, and Roger Lundin

The Black Church and Hip Hop Culture: Toward Bridging the Generational Divide edited by Emmett G. Price III

Culture Care: Reconnecting with Beauty for Our Common Life by Makoto Fujimura

Multicultural Ministry Handbook: Connecting Creatively to a Diverse World edited by David A. Anderson and Margarita R. Cabellon

Reconciling All Things: A Christian Vision for Justice, Peace and Healing by Emmanuel Katongole and Chris Rice

ACKNOWLEDGMENTS

This book is the product of a great cloud of ethnicity-aware witnesses who encouraged, advised, and partnered with me; told me I wasn't crazy; and believed in this book more than me at times. Without their own examples of faithfulness and courage in the multiethnic journey, we wouldn't have this book!

To my editor Al Hsu, Helen Lee, and the InterVarsity Press staff, thank you for your patience, wise guidance, believing in this book, and persevering with me in its many turns.

To the many women and men who were willing to share their stories, thank you for your gift of love to me and the many who will read this book. Your stories help this book come to life, giving it so much more texture, variety, and embodied hope than I could on my own. May the Lord bless your freely given offering.

To Chris Nichols, thank you for encouraging me to write this book and giving me space to do so. This would have never happened without you. I'm grateful for how you, as a white man, make space for me and so many leaders of color.

To the venerable Dr. Emmett Price III and Dr. Virginia Ward, thank you for your wisdom, mentorship, and advocacy in my life and in this book. I and so many others are indebted to the gracious and prophetic voices of black spiritual leaders like you. Thank you for embracing all of who I am in my ethnicity and my leadership.

To Dr. James Choung, I'm indebted to you for many things. It was you who first helped me see that I could be a Korean American, woman, Christian leader. Your example of ethnicity-aware leadership helped me not give up on Jesus or our people. And without the evangelistic framework you developed for sharing the gospel, I wouldn't have been able to develop the ideas in this book. Thank you for your manifold influence of good fruit in my life.

To Dr. Jeff Liou, thank you for always being willing to lend your ear and wisdom to this Asian American sister.

To Doug Schaupp and Maureen Huang, thank you for believing in me and being the best cheerleaders and partners in ministry anyone could ask for. As white leaders, you use your voice, influence, and leadership to make room for so many others.

To my colleagues in the Multiethnic Ministries department of InterVarsity, you have taught me so much about the beauty of our multiethnic family. Thank you for your prayers, support, and partnership.

To Andrew Givens, Brent Campbell, Julie Day, Kelly Joiner, Jeremy Ogunba, Megan Krischke, Kaitlin Ho, and so many others who led in reconciliation and witness with me, thank you for inspiring me with your courageous leadership in mission and trusting me in the journey.

To countless friends, colleagues, and my church family, thank you for praying for me and this book. To the pastors at Highrock Covenant Church, your commitment to loving the other is beautiful to behold.

To my parents, Q and Kyung Shin, thank you for teaching me that my ethnicity is beautiful and for always encouraging me to dream and lead.

To my in-laws KH and Euiju Maeng, thank you for loving and supporting me like your own daughter.

And to the real MVP, my husband Shin Maeng, thank you for cheering for me and putting up with my countless hours and days of writing, speaking, and traveling. Your love for me and for people of every ethnicity helps me stay the course on this journey every day.

Finally, to Jesus, the great author of every ethnic story and reconciler of all things. Thank you for giving us a story too beautiful to be left untold.

NOTES

CHAPTER 1: BEYOND COLORBLIND

[1]Desmond Tutu and John Hope Franklin, "A Journey Towards Peace," PBS interview, February 9, 2001, www.pbs.org/journeytopeace/meettutu/future.html.

[2]Naomi Murakawa, *The First Civil Right: How Liberals Built Prison America* (New York: Oxford University Press, 2014), 7.

[3]Michelle Alexander, *The New Jim Crow: Mass Incarceration in the Age of Colorblindness* (New York: The New Press, 2012), 179.

[4]Desmond Tutu, "Ten Pieces of Wisdom from Desmond Tutu to Inspire Change Makers in 2016," Desmond Tutu Peace Foundation, January 3, 2016, www.tutufoundationusa.org/2016/01/03/ten-quotes-from-desmond-tutu-to-inspire-change-makers-in-2016.

[5]Oscar Wilde, *The Complete Works of Oscar Wilde*, ed. Russell Jackson and Ian Small (Oxford: Oxford University Press, 2005), 126.

[6]United States Census Bureau, "About Hispanic Origin," January 26, 2017, www.census.gov/topics/population/hispanic-origin/about.html.

[7]Though ethnic stories also intersect with and are affected by our gender and sexuality, we will be focusing on ethnicity for the purposes of this book.

[8]James Choung, *True Story* (Downers Grove, IL: InterVarsity Press, 2008), 205-18.

CHAPTER 2: ETHNICITIES MADE FOR GOOD

[1]Soong-Chan Rah, *The Next Evangelicalism* (Downers Grove, IL: InterVarsity Press, 2009), 33.

[2]Richard Twiss, *Rescuing the Gospel from the Cowboys* (Downers Grove, IL: InterVarsity Press, 2015), 125.

CHAPTER 3: THE CRACKS IN OUR ETHNICITY

[1]"Asian American Teenage Girls Have Highest Rates of Depression," National Alliance on Mental Illness, January 1, 2011, www.nami.org /press-Media/press-releases/2011/asian-american-teenage-girls-have -highest-rates-of#sthash.1b1W6nP4.dpuf.

[2]"Suicide Among Asian Americans," Asian American Psychological Association, May 2012, https://aapaonline.org/wp-content/uploads/2014/06 /AAPA-suicide-factsheet.pdf.

[3]Krishna Ramanujan, "Health Expert Explains Asian and Asian-American Students' Unique Pressures to Succeed," *Cornell Chronicle*, April 19, 2006, www.news.cornell.edu/stories/2006/04/health-expert-explains-asian -students-unique-pressures-succeed.

[4]Miroslav Volf, *Exclusion and Embrace: A Theological Exploration of Identity, Otherness, and Reconciliation* (Nashville: Abingdon Press, 1996), 81.

[5]Hansi Lo Wang, "'Awoken' By N.Y. Cop Shooting, Asian-American Activists Chart Way Forward," *Code Switch*, NPR, April 23, 2016, www.npr .org/sections/codeswitch/2016/04/23/475369524/awoken-by-n-y-cop -shooting-asian-american-activists-chart-way-forward.

[6]Michelle Alexander, *The New Jim Crow: Mass Incarceration in the Age of Colorblindness* (New York: The New Press, 2012), 6, 7, 98.

[7]Lynn Langton and Matthew R. Durose, "Police Behavior During Traffic and Street Stops, 2011," Bureau of Justice Statistics, September 24, 2013, www.bjs.gov/index.cfm?ty=pbdetail&iid=4779; and Sharon LaFraniere and Andrew W. Lehren, "The Disproportionate Risks of Driving While Black," *New York Times*, October 24, 2015, www.nytimes.com/2015/10/25/us/racial -disparity-traffic-stops-driving-black.html.

[8]"Mental Health and African Americans," U.S. Department of Health and Human Services Office of Minority Mental Health, http://minorityhealth.hhs .gov/omh/browse.aspx?lvl=4&lvlid=24; and Vickie M. Mays, Susan D. Cochran, and Namdi W. Barnes, "Race, Race-Based Discrimination, and Health Outcomes Among African Americans," *Annual Review of Psychology* 58 (January 2007): 201-25, www.ncbi.nlm.nih.gov/pmc/articles/PMC4181672/.

[9]Mark Charles, Wirelesshogan, www.wirelesshogan.com.

[10]This form follows the well-known prayer Teresa of Avila wrote of her difficulty in trying to truly love God: "Oh God, I don't love you, I don't even want to love you, but I want to want to love you."

CHAPTER 4: ETHNICITIES
RESTORED FOR BETTER

[1]Richard Twiss, *Rescuing the Gospel from the Cowboys* (Downers Grove, IL: InterVarsity Press, 2015), 116.

[2]Ibid., 186.

[3]Levi Coffin, *Reminiscences of Levi Coffin, the Reputed President of the Underground Railroad* (Cincinnati: Robert Clarke & Co.: 1880), 108.

[4]"Rwanda's Grass Courts," *New York Times*, July 10, 2004, www.nytimes .com/2004/07/10/opinion/rwanda-s-grass-courts.html.

[5]For more on Antione's powerful story, see Antoine Rutayisire, *Faith Under Fire: Testimonies of Christian Bravery* (African Enterprise, 1973).

[6]Corrie ten Boom with Elizabeth and John Sherrill, *The Hiding Place*, 35th anniversary ed. (Grand Rapids: Chosen Books, 2006), 247-48.

[7]Caroline Praderio, "One Man Has Spent Years Befriending KKK Members and Persuaded 200 of Them to Leave the Hate Group," *Business Insider*, December 28, 2016, www.businessinsider.com/daryl-davis-making-friends -with-kkk-documentary-2016-12.

[8]Joan Chittister, *God's Tender Mercy* (New London, CT: Twenty-Third Productions, 2010), 66.

[9]Miroslav Volf, *Exclusion and Embrace: A Theological Exploration of Identity, Otherness, and Reconciliation* (Nashville: Abingdon Press, 1996), 124.

CHAPTER 5: REDEEMED ETHNIC
IDENTITIES SENT OUT TO HEAL

[1]Amy-Jill Levine, "Visions of Kingdoms," ed. Michael D. Coogan, *The Oxford History of the Biblical World* (New York: Oxford University Press, 1998), 366.

[2]InterVarsity Twentyonehundred Productions, "Brent Campbell, Staff Conference 2014," https://vimeo.com/83792223.

[3]Martin Luther King Jr., "Pilgrimage to Nonviolence," in *A Testament of Hope: The Essential Writing and Speeches of Martin Luther King Jr.*, ed. James M. Washington (New York: Harper Collins, 1986), 38.

[4]Jorge Maldonado, Greg Yee, and Kurt Peterson, "Strength Through Diversity," The Evangelical Covenant Church, www.covchurch.org/history/ diversity.

[5]Mellody Hobson, "Be Color Brave, Not Color Blind," TED Blog, March 20, 2014, http://blog.ted.com/be-color-brave-not-color-blind-mellody-hobson-at-ted2014/.

[6]Carol Dweck, "The Power of Believing That You Can Improve," TED Talk, December 2014, www.ted.com/talks/carol_dweck_the_power_of_believing _that_you_can_improve/transcript?language=en.

CHAPTER 6: TRUST-BUILDING WITH ETHNIC STRANGERS

[1]Don Everts and Doug Schaupp, *I Once Was Lost* (Downers Grove, IL: Inter-Varsity Press, 2008), 36-38.

[2]Eugene A. Nida, *Fascinated by Languages* (Philadelphia: John Benjamins Publishing Company, 2003), 30.

[3]Offensive terms span many different ethnic groups: *nigger* for black Americans, *chink* for Chinese or Asian Americans, *redskin* for Native Americans, *wetback* for Latino Americans, *guido* for Italian Americans, among others. This list can go on.

[4]Christena Cleveland, *Disunity in Christ* (Downers Grove, IL: InterVarsity Press, 2013), 61.

CHAPTER 7: CROSSCULTURAL SKILLS IN COMMUNITY

[1]David A. Livermore, *Cultural Intelligence* (Grand Rapids: Baker Academic, 2009), 19.

[2]Ibid., 63.

[3]"Connecticut Profile," Prison Policy Initiative (Northampton, MA), accessed June 16, 2017, www.prisonpolicy.org/profiles/CT.html.

CHAPTER 8: RESPONDING TO CROSSCULTURAL CONFLICT IN COMMUNITY

[1]The Situation-Behavior-Impact tool was developed by the Center for Creative Leadership (www.ccl.org) and is widely used in leadership and management coaching.

[2]Brenda Salter McNeil, *Roadmap to Reconciliation* (Downers Grove, IL: InterVarsity Press, 2015), 83.

CHAPTER 9: PROPHETIC ETHNIC JUSTICE

[1] Martin Luther King Jr., "Pilgrimage to Nonviolence," in *A Testament of Hope: The Essential Writing and Speeches of Martin Luther King Jr.*, ed. James M. Washington (New York: Harper Collins, 1986), 37.

[2] Nicholas Wolterstorff, *Justice: Rights and Wrongs* (Princeton, NJ: Princeton University Press, 2008), 110-13.

[3] For more about racial segregation after the Federal Housing Act, see Kenneth T. Jackson, "Race, Ethnicity, and the Real Estate Appraisal: The Home Owners Loan Corporation and the Federal Housing Administration," by *Journal of Urban History* 6, no. 4 (August 1980); and Natasha M. Trifun, "Residential Segregation After the Fair Housing Act," *Human Rights* magazine, vol. 36, no. 4, www.americanbar.org/publications/human_rights_magazine_home/human_rights_vol36_2009/fall2009/residential_segregation_after_the_fair_housing_act.html.

[4] "The House We Live In," *Race, the Power of an Illusion*, PBS, episode 3.

[5] Ibid.

[6] N. T. Wright, *Evil and the Justice of God* (Downers Grove, IL: InterVarsity Press, 2006), 64.

[7] Brenda Salter McNeil, *Roadmap to Reconciliation* (Downers Grove, IL: InterVarsity Press, 2015), 22.

[8] See Ta-Nehisi Coates, "The Case for Reparations," *The Atlantic*, June 2014, www.theatlantic.com/magazine/archive/2014/06/the-case-for-reparations/361631/, for an argument for reparations.

[9] F. F. Bruce, *New Testament History* (New York: Doubleday, 1969), 40.

[10] J. A. Motyer and G. J. Wenham, eds., "Cleansing of the Temple," *New Bible Commentary* (Downers Grove, IL: IVP Academic, 2007), 1030.

[11] Michelle Alexander, *The New Jim Crow* (New York: The New Press, 2012), 180.

CHAPTER 10: CULTURE RE-CREATORS

[1] Andy Crouch, *Culture Making: Recovering Our Creative Calling* (Downers Grove, IL: InterVarsity Press, 2008), 90-98.

[2] Traci G. Lee: "The Rise, Fall, and Rise Again of MC Jin," NBC News, April 9, 2015, www.nbcnews.com/news/asian-america/return-mc-jin-n324236.

[3] Lamin Sanneh, *Translating the Message* (Marynoll, NY: Orbis Books, 1989), 200, 208.

[4]Lamin Sanneh, *Disciples of All Nations: Pillars of World Christianity* (New York: Oxford University Press, 2008), xxiii.

[5]Makoto Fujimura, "What Do You Want to Make Today?," Biola University, 2012 commencement address, www.makotofujimura.com/writings/what -do-you-want-to-make-today/.

ABOUT THE AUTHOR

Sarah Shin is on staff with InterVarsity Christian Fellowship and serves as associate national director of evangelism. She has trained college ministry professionals and college students across the country in crosscultural skills and ethnicity awareness, connecting ethnic identity awareness, reconciliation, and evangelism. Sarah is a speaker, writer, artist, and trainer, and she has helped develop leaders in both ethnic-specific and multiethnic contexts.

Before serving in ministry, Sarah earned a master's degree in city planning from the Massachusetts Institute of Technology in Cambridge, Massachusetts, and then worked as a city planner, helping create neighborhood revitalization plans and master plans for city redevelopment in the United States and overseas. While volunteering with InterVarsity, she realized that she loved seeing the lights go on when someone understands more about God, so she's been doing college ministry ever since. Sarah also has a master's degree in theology from Gordon-Conwell Theological Seminary.

Sarah and her husband, Shin Maeng, live in Cambridge, Massachusetts, and they love to paint, eat, host, and welcome strangers into the city together.

INTERVARSITY
INTERVARSITY CHRISTIAN FELLOWSHIP/USA

InterVarsity Christian Fellowship/USA is a movement of students and faculty active on almost seven hundred college and university campuses across the nation. InterVarsity has an estimated one million alumni as a result of its seventy-five–year history. The vision of InterVarsity is to see the transformation of students and faculty, the development of world-changers, and the renewal of campuses. In response to God's love, grace, and truth, InterVarsity establishes and advances witnessing communities that follow Jesus as Savior and Lord; growing in love for God, God's Word, God's people of every ethnicity and culture, and God's purposes in the world.

InterVarsity's core values include Scripture, prayer, spiritual formation, community, discipleship of the mind, leadership development, evangelism, whole life stewardship, ethnic reconciliation and justice, church, and missions. As an expression of these values, InterVarsity hosts Urbana, a student missions conference, held every three years since 1946. Urbana has challenged more than three hundred thousand participants to accept the responsibility and privilege of engaging in global missions. InterVarsity Press, an extension of InterVarsity, is a leading Christian publisher with a respected history of providing resources that strengthen the church, encourage individuals, and shape the academy.

InterVarsity's ministry is strategic because universities have a significant influence on the broader culture. More than that, InterVarsity is present on campus to reveal the love and hope of Jesus and to develop men and women spiritually so they might spend a lifetime serving his purposes and then dwell with God for all of eternity.

Learn more at www.intervarsity.org.